BUSINESS SERVING RURAL MIDWEST COMMUNITIES

Carol R. Turner

ABSTRACT

The rural Midwest region of the United States serves as a significant locus

for American history, culture, and faith, in addition to being renowned as the

nation's primary agricultural hub for maize and soybeans production.

Nevertheless, the prevailing body of literature pertaining to the integration

of business and Christian ministry for the common good predominantly

represented the viewpoints of individuals engaged in international missions

or those involved in urban settings regarding the underlying purposes of

business. Limited knowledge existed regarding the practices and perceptions

of business as ministry stakeholders in the rural Midwestern United States

concerning the concept of the common good. In order to bridge this

knowledge gap, the present dissertation employed a basic qualitative

research methodology to gather data from a sample of 33 stakeholders

representing 14 businesses as Christian ministries, such as farms and small

enterprises, situated in the rural region of Iowa, United States. The

fundamental understanding of this study was that stakeholders in the rural

Midwestern United States who supported business as ministry believed that

the organization possesses spiritual, social, intellectual, and financial capital

resources that could be utilized for the common good. The present

exposition of the common good treasure concept and the business as

ministry model is based on well-established scholarly literature, recognized

qualitative research methodologies, and the findings derived from the data

analysis of this basic qualitative research. Based on the common good treasure concept and the business as ministry model, a purpose and resource-based analysis methodology was developed for business as ministry. This methodology offers valuable insights into the optimization of the common good treasure to achieve sustainable entrepreneurial and ministerial outcomes for business as ministry. The practical implications of this study, as well as the common good treasure concept and the business as ministry model, may aid Christian entrepreneurs in comprehending and managing a business as a Christian ministry. Furthermore, this research has made a significant contribution to the foundation for developing a potential theory of business as ministry, which could include an analysis of its purpose, resources, and market.

Table of Contents

Table of Contents

Chapter 1

Introduction

Human activity is not the sum of each human being's efforts but rather an integrative human collective endeavor. Integration includes human-to-human interaction, human-to-creator interaction, and human-to-nature interaction. As a result, humans live not only for their benefit but also for the honor of their creator, community, and nature, i.e., the common good of humanity.

This study aimed to gain a comprehensive understanding of the perceptions and interpretations of the common good held by rural entrepreneurs in the Midwestern region of the United States who operate their businesses with a Christian ministry approach. The region commonly referred to as the Midwest in the United States is widely recognized as the nation's heartland, representing a significant hub of American history, culture, and religious beliefs. Native Americans have inhabited the land for a significant time spanning thousands of years. The name of the State of Iowa can be traced back to its origins in the Ioway tribe of Native Americans (Cayton et al., 2006). Since the 1800s, there has been a significant migration of Europeans from the East of America and Europe directly to the US Midwest. This migration has resulted in the establishment of generations of US Midwestern Christian entrepreneurs. Examples include the Lutheran Hollanders in Pella,

Iowa, Catholics in Dubuque, Iowa, Congregationalists and Presbyterians in the southeast Iowa town of Denmark, Methodists in Dubuque, Iowa, Amish in Kalona and Leon, southeast Iowa, and Quakers in West Branch and New Providence, Iowa (Schwieder et al., 2002). These entrepreneurs have encountered specific challenges in integrating business and ministry for the common good.

Ancient philosophy and early Christianity are the antecedents of the concept of the common good. According to the Aristotelian-Thomistic philosophical tradition, the highest good of humanity and the good of each citizen is the common good, and citizenship allows people to engage in and contribute to the common good (Sison & Fontrodona, 2012). As a Christian philosopher, Aquinas incorporated God into the Aristotelian concept of the common good by suggesting God as the common good of all (Sison & Fontrodona, 2011).

Business as ministry is known as a profit-making business that promotes human flourishing by stewarding all of God's resources to meet the needs of the created world and convening the needs of stakeholders through Christ-like business practices (C. N. Johnson, 2009; Rundle & Steffen, 2003; Van Duzer, 2010). A business as ministry serves the common good (Lindblad, 2016) financially through self-sustainable financial support, spiritually through the reconciliation of the God-human relationship, socially through the restoration of the human-human relationship, and ecologically through the refurbishment of the human-nature relationship.

Currently, the majority of literature on the common good and business as ministry focused on overseas missions and urban practices concerning the purpose of business

(Banks & Stevens, 2005; Befus, 2002; Felber, 2019; McVea & Naughton, 2021; Stolze, 2021). In the Midwest, the heartland of America, farmers cultivate copious grain crops, such as corn, soybean, wheat, and oats, due to the region's fertile soils. Despite their diverse Christian faith traditions and cultural heritage, many Christian farmers and small business entrepreneurs in the Midwestern United States engaged in business as ministry. As a researcher with a background as a Christian urban farmer, I was interested in how the business as ministry stakeholders in the rural Midwestern United States practiced and perceived business as ministry for the common good.

Problem Statement

Presently, the prevailing body of literature pertaining to business as ministry and the common good predominantly represented the viewpoints of individuals engaged in international missions or those involved in urban settings regarding the underlying purposes of business. Limited knowledge existed regarding how the business as ministry stakeholders in the rural Midwestern United States practiced and perceived business as ministry for the common good.

Purpose Statement

This basic qualitative study aimed to understand how the business as ministry stakeholders in the rural Midwestern United States practiced and perceived business as ministry for the common good.

Research Questions

The principal question of this research was "How do the business as ministry stakeholders in the rural Midwestern United States practice and perceive business as ministry for the common good?"

There were five sub-questions:

1. How do they practice and perceive the financial aspects of business as ministry for the common good?

2. How do they practice and perceive the spiritual aspects of business as ministry for the common good?

3. How do they practice and perceive the social aspects of business as ministry for the common good?

4. How do they practice and perceive the intellectual aspects of business as ministry for the common good?

5. What other practices and perceptions do they hold about their business as ministry for the common good?

Definitions

For this study, the following definitions were used.

Business as ministry—a profit-making business as a Christian ministry with the belief that God can utilize businesses to further His purposes on earth (New International Version Bible, 2011/1973, Colossians 3:23–24, Matthew 25:14–30). Business as ministry serves the common good when done well and sustainably (Lindblad, 2016).

Business as mission—this concept was established in 1999 at the Oxford Center for Mission Studies to define a global Christian missional strategy of using business as a vehicle to reach the world's least-resourced and least-reached regions. (N. Johnson & Rundle, 2006).

Family social capital—the network of social interactions characterized by goodwill and trust that exist among families who run businesses (Sorenson & Milbrandt, 2023).

Nature versus nurture—The debate surrounding the respective influences of genetic factors (nature) and environmental factors (nurture) on an individual's development. Nativists prioritize the influence of genetics, while environmentalists prioritize societal and ecological elements, such as family views, child-rearing methods, and economic position (American Psychological Association, n.d.).

Stakeholders—Shareholders, employees, customers, and vendors of the business, as well as fellowships and churches who support or are involved in the ministry (Van Duzer, 2010).

The common good—Thomas Aquinas (1950) posited that God is the overall common good. Hussain (2018) denotes the common good as those materials, cultural or institutional facilities that the society provides to all members to accomplish a relational duty and care for specific interests they have in common.

Scope

The scope of my research was confined to a sample of 33 stakeholders, who were selected to represent 14 enterprises operating in the rural region of Iowa, United States of America. The prerequisite for business ownership entails adhering to the Christian faith and adopting a mindset that views business as a Christian ministry. There were no limitations imposed on the scale or nature of enterprises. The enterprises functioned within the rural regions of the US Midwest. They had implemented business as ministry for at least five years to establish the study's trustworthiness. As for stakeholders other than the owners, the requirement is involvement in business as ministry in rural Midwestern United States without regard to a particular faith tradition.

Limitations

The transferability limitations may arise from the specific focus of my research on a rural area in the Midwest, USA. The sample might not evenly represent each type of stakeholder, as family members operated most family farms. There might be limitations in distinguishing between the owners and the workers and between the employers and the employees. Furthermore, as an academic researcher from an Asian American Christian cultural background and possessing an urban farmer's viewpoint, I may have difficulties fully comprehending the intricacies of the practices and

perceptions held by the US rural

Midwestern participants.

Significance Statement

The fundamental understanding of this study was that stakeholders in

the rural Midwestern United States who supported business as ministry

believed that the organization possesses spiritual, social, intellectual, and

financial capital resources that could be utilized for the common good. The

present exposition of the common good treasure concept and the business as

ministry model is based on well-established scholarly literature, recognized

qualitative research methodologies, and the findings derived from the data

analysis of this basic qualitative research. Based on the common good

treasure concept and the business as ministry model, a purpose and resource-

based analysis methodology was developed for business as ministry. This

methodology offers valuable insights into the optimization of the common

good treasure to achieve sustainable entrepreneurial and ministerial outcomes

for business as ministry. The practical implications of this study, as well as

the common good treasure concept and the business as ministry model, may

aid

Christian entrepreneurs in comprehending and managing a business as a

Christian ministry. Furthermore, this research has made a significant

contribution to the foundation for developing a potential theory of business as

ministry, which could include an analysis of its

purpose, resources, and market.

Chapter 2

Literature Review

The purpose of this basic qualitative study is to understand how business as ministry stakeholders in the US rural Midwest practice and perceive the common good. This chapter examines four major areas related to the research questions in order to comprehend the context of this study. The first section gives background regarding the history, culture, and faith traditions of the rural Midwest of the United States. The second section provides an overview of the literature about the common good related to business. The third section introduces various business models. The final section investigates the literature on business as ministry.

The US Rural Midwest

The US Midwest is also known as the American heartland, consisting of 12 states in the North Central Region of the USA (Census History Staff, 2023). They are the five Old Northwest states (Wisconsin, Michigan, Illinois, Indiana, and Ohio) and the seven states with tallgrass prairie (Iowa, Minnesota, Missouri, Nebraska, Kansas, North and South Dakotas) (Steiner, 2018). The Corn Belt is another name for the rural Midwest, representing the farming and agriculture in the area, which has level land, rich, deep soils, and a significant amount of organic soil for the cultivation of corn and soybeans as the feed-grains for livestock. The Corn Belt is the world's most productive region regarding biological production during the growing season (Guanter et al., 2014; Morello, 2014; Schultz, 2014). Most of the farms in the rural Midwest are family-run, with an average size of more than 300 acres (Britannica, n.d.). Today, around one-third of all rural midwestern acreage is used for soybean production because planting soybeans can aid in fertilizing the soil with nitrogen, a major nutrient needed for corn. Thus, the Corn-Soybean Belt should be the new moniker for this area (Cayton et al., 2006).

History

Iowa is one of the major states in the Corn-Soybean Belt, characterizing the rural Midwest in history. American Indians have inhabited the area for thousands of years. The state's name, Iowa, derives from the American Indian Ioway tribe (Schwieder et al., 2002).

Since the migration of Europeans from the East of America and Europe directly to the Midwest in the 1800s, the generations of Midwestern Christian entrepreneurs have encountered specific challenges in their integration of business and Christian ministry for the common good. According to the Census of 1870, the total state population of Iowa was 1,194,020, with a total foreign-born population of 204,692. Among the foreign-born population, 32% were from Germany, 20% from Ireland, 12% from Great Britain, 9% from British America, 9% from Norway, 5% from Sweden, 3% from Bohemia, 2% from Holland, 2% from Switzerland, 2% from France, etc. (Schwieder et al., 2002, p. 44). Most pioneers migrated to Iowa because they knew "they could buy good land for little money" (Schwieder et al., 2002, p.

44). In the 1830s and 1840s, farmlands were sold to the early settlers with 80 acres for US$100 to each family. At the time, US$100 represented several years' worth of savings from work for some families (Schwieder et al., 2002). Although the land was cheap and fertile, there was a lack of timber and fear of prairie fire raging across the dry grasslands. It was not an easy task to build a shelter without enough wood. Despite being difficult, pioneer life in Iowa did not feel isolated. Since farms were close to one another, "a good deal of visiting went on" (Schwieder et al., 2002, p. 58).

Culture

The rural Midwestern culture was shaped largely by immigrants and the natural environment (Danbom, 2014). The Puritans, who emigrated from England to New England of America in 1630, were strongly committed to education. There were two components to the culture of education. The Bible, which they believed to be God's word, was the first book they believed everyone should read. They also thought that learning to read increased people's desire to work. Laziness was considered a sin by the Puritans, and not working was considered to be lazy. Life was particularly challenging in the Midwest's early settlement's chilly winters. There were some shelters without hardwood floors. Pioneer women often had to stand on a wood block to complete household chores. In this context, the culture of hard-working and neighborliness gradually began to take root (Schwieder et al., 2002). Hurt (2014) described the rural Midwestern culture as "independent, egalitarian, and democratic"; it existed distant from the metropolis, which the

Midwesterners viewed as "corrupt, violent, and poverty-stricken" (p. 1). Hurt used imagery from the works of Midwestern artists such as Grant Wood, John Steuart Curry, and Thomas Hart Benton to demonstrate how the idea of the Midwest as a moral and ethical ideal persisted into the twenty-first century. Rural Midwesterners lived peaceful, secure, and well-ordered lives with small-town family values, dedication to hard work, and cooperative efforts, which provided economic, social, and political stability as the cornerstone for a strong nation. Life in the rural Midwest was an example of American culture with a benevolent nature (Hurt,

2014).

Hurt (2014) also discussed the newest cultural theory of biological interconnectedness in nature, which ecologist Aldo Leopold supported with a term called "land ethic," referring to the "community" inside an ecosystem (p. 1). In this ecosystem, the land produces a "cultural harvest" that may be used to educate people about their relationship to nature, the land, and the values that can be applied to rural life in the

Midwest while practicing good land management to avoid mistreating the soil.

Additionally, Leopold proposed an association between "absolute harmony with the land" and "absolute justice and liberty" (Hurt, 2014, p. 2).

On the other hand, David Danbom (2014), contended that technology continues to play a role in transforming rural cultural patterns by enabling fewer and fewer farmers to work in larger and larger areas. Depopulation and falling family sizes caused farm consolidation, along with school and church consolidation, which made it more challenging to retain the regional customs and institutions that had shaped the distinctive neighborhood culture. Farm women were no longer bound to domestic duties and could now seek outside jobs for a wage, acting more like non-farm women (Sano & Fujita, 2006). Danbom (2014) argued that "farming had become a technologically sophisticated business, and farmers were increasingly embracing a modern, urban material culture" (p. 300).

Faith

The cheap land enchanted early European immigrants in the United States. Religious issues were another factor in the exodus from Europe. They knew they could create a new church or attend any church they chose in the United States. For instances, many people left Sweden in the middle of the 1800s because they disagreed with Lutheran authorities on paying church taxes. Around 800 people fled Holland in 1847 because they did not want to be a part of the state church. Hollanders established the community of Pella in Iowa, where they could practice their religion freely (Schwieder et al., 2002). Every nation in Europe had a state church, much like Sweden. Regardless of their religious beliefs, all residents paid taxes to fund the state church.

Because diverse religious groups migrating from Europe to America opposed paying taxes to support other clergies, the United States Constitution's authors chose to try having no official state church. In other words, all churches are equal, and Americans are free to attend whichever church they want or none at all. The term "religious freedom" refers to this ideology. The state will not get involved or favor one faith over another. It was called the separation of church and state (Vile et al., 2008). I shall explore the contributions of various ethnic groups to the culture of this context.

The city, Dubuque, has played a significant role in Catholic life since the earliest American settlers arrived in Iowa. Catholic Irish miners worked in the lead mines close to the city. Father Samuel Mazzuchelli, a priest from Italy, traveled to Dubuque to serve those people. In the 1830s, he assisted in constructing St. Raphael's church and seven other Catholic churches (Schwieder et al., 2002). In contrast to Catholics, Congregationalists felt that each congregation should be in charge of its own affairs and not be governed by a bishop. Many Congregationalists descended from the New England Puritans. Due to their shared religious values, Presbyterians and Congregationalists frequently attended services together on the frontier. They occasionally cast votes to unite as a single church. In 1838, the first Congregational Church was founded in the southeast Iowa town of Denmark (Schwieder et al., 2002). The Iowa Band, made up of eleven Massachusetts college students, was formed in 1843 in response to Reverend Asa Turner's request to serve as missionaries in the Midwest. The Methodist Church was the biggest faith group in frontier Iowa. In Dubuque in 1834, Methodists constructed their first chapel. Visiting new settlers on the frontier required Methodist circuit riders to ride horses. On the frontier, the Methodist Church grew remarkably steadfast. With 90,000 members by the Civil War, it had become Iowa's largest church (Schwieder et al., 2002).

The Community of True Inspiration originated in Germany in the early 1700s. A group of people who belonged to the Lutheran Church wanted a simpler faith since they thought they had received messages or inspiration from God. The group's leaders departed the Lutheran Church with other Inspirationists after putting the messages down on paper as their religious convictions. The Inspirationists were mistreated and prohibited from purchasing land in Germany. The group decided to immigrate to America in search of freedom and land. Christian Metz led the group as they fled from Germany to America (Szabados, 2021). Later, some of them relocated to Iowa. Today, there are eight villages in the community known as Amana ("remain faithful") in eastern Iowa (Schwieder et al., 2002, pp. 187–188). Inspirationists lead humble lives in the Amana communities. All participants wear simple, black attire. Families reside in residences provided by church authorities rather than their own homes. There are no kitchens in Amana homes. In a few big kitchens, people share the common good. Each kitchen serves about forty people. The Amana people adhere to practicing their faith in all aspects of life. They think it is selfish for people to think about themselves solely. Instead, everyone should consider how they might honor God and benefit one another (Schwieder et al., 2002), the common good to all.

In the 1800s, as a prominent part of the abolitionist movements, numerous Quaker settlements, including West Branch and New Providence in Iowa, relocated from the US South to the Midwest (Schwieder et al., 2002). According to the US census in 1850, in terms of a state's total accommodations, 2.1% in Ohio, 1.2% in Minnesota, 6.3% in Indiana, and 3.6% in Iowa were Quakers (Barlow & Silk, 2004, p. 69). George Fox founded the Quaker Movement, generally known as the Religious Society of Friends, in England in the 17th century. Along with other early Quakers or Friends, he was persecuted for his ideas, which included the notion that the presence of God dwells in every person as the "Inner Light." Quakers disapproved of complex religious rituals lacked an official clergy and believed in spiritual equality for men and women. Midway through the 1650s, the initial Quaker missionaries arrived in America. Quakers, who embrace pacifism, were instrumental in both the abolitionist and the women's rights movements (A&E Television Networks, 2023).

The Amish community was established in the 1690s by Mennonite minister Jakob Ammann in Switzerland (Nolt, 2016). In the 1840s, the Old Order Amish relocated to Iowa from Pennsylvania. They are frequently referred to as the "horse and buggy people" since they don't drive cars, and they are also occasionally referred to as "plain people" because of the way they dress (Schwieder et al., 2002, p. 195). The Old Order Amish refused to adopt new technologies and fashion trends. They thought God wanted them to continue living the way they had in the past and that everyone should dress alike so that others might easily identify them as Amish.

Additionally, they strongly believed that all Amish people should live on farms rather than in cities and towns (Schwieder et al., 2002). Due to their desire for cars and telephones, another Amish group, the Beachy Amish, broke away from the Old Order in the 1920s. Although they live in a more contemporary fashion, the Beachy Amish share many religious beliefs with the Old Order. Beachy Amish families may own automobiles, but they must be black. While the Old Order continues to farm like many Iowans farmed in the 1920s, the Beachy Amish homes are electrified with contemporary technology. About one-fifth of the Amish in Iowa today is Beachy, and they reside close to Kalona and Leon, Iowa. Amish attitudes regarding education are influenced by their religious beliefs. They firmly feel that eight years of education is sufficient for their children. Then, Amish parents instruct their kids at home in subjects like agricultural and domestic vocational training. Amish parents worry that their kids won't want to be Amish when they graduate high school or college (Schwieder et al., 2002).

The Catholic Worker Movement was founded in New York City in 1933 under the joint leadership of Dorothy Day and Peter Maurin. The movement was founded upon the fundamental tenets of nonviolence, voluntary poverty, and the Works of Mercy. Catholic Workers adhere to the belief that they have a moral obligation to actively demonstrate solidarity with individuals who are poor and socially excluded while also actively advocating for equitable social conditions (Loughery, 2020; Zwick, 2005).

The Catholic Worker Movement was introduced to the state of Iowa during

the early 1940s. In 1941, Dorothy Day and Peter Maurin visited Iowa City,

where they delivered lectures. In the subsequent year, a Catholic Worker

residence was established in Iowa City. The establishment of the Catholic

Worker House in Iowa City marked an early expansion of Catholic Worker

houses beyond the confines of New York City. During the 1950s and

1960s, there was a notable growth and expansion of the Catholic Worker
Movement in

Iowa. Catholic Worker residences were established in Des Moines, Waterloo,

and Cedar Rapids. Catholic Workers residing in Iowa actively engaged in

numerous social justice movements, encompassing the civil rights movement,

the anti-war movement, and the farmworkers' movement (Miller, 1984;

Piehl, 1988).

Summary of the US Rural Midwest

The rural Midwest region in the United States, known for its

exceptional biological productivity (Morello, 2014), is characterized by a

unique culture that sets it apart from other regions globally. The rural

Midwestern culture has had significant influence from both the inhabitants

and the ecological characteristics of the prairieland. Bowring et al. (2015)

found a favorable correlation between biodiversity and bioproductivity, as per

their research conducted at Massachusetts Institute of Technology. The

establishment of diverse freedoms in speech, worship, want, and fear under

the United States Constitution has facilitated the coexistence and collaboration of indigenous populations and immigrants from many countries of origin, resulting in a cohesive and productive society for the common good. The history, culture, and faith of the US rural Midwesterners exemplified the spirit and the essence of a diversified and yet united states of America, the spirit of the

common good.

The Common Good of Business

In contrast to "me the selfish jerk seeking as much wealth and power as possible" (Reich, 2018, p. 13), the US Constitution was deliberated for "we the people" seeking to "promote the general welfare," the common good. It resonated with Franklin D. Roosevelt's "Four Freedoms—freedom of speech, of worship, freedom from want, and freedom from fear" (Reich, 2018, p. 13). Hussain (2018) denoted the common good as those materials, cultural or institutional facilities that the society provides to all members to accomplish a relational duty and care for specific interests they have in common. This section will review the history of the concept of the common good and the Catholic, protestants', and scientific perspectives of the common good.

A Brief History of the Common Good Concept Development

The historical roots of the common good can be found in early Christianity and ancient philosophy (Sison & Fontrodona, 2012). In the Aristotelian–Thomistic philosophical tradition, the concept of the common good has long been an area of study and practice. For Aristotle, the common good is man's highest good and the good of every citizen. Through

citizenship, people contribute to the common good (Sison & Fontrodona,

2012). As a Christian philosopher, Thomas Aquinas integrated God into the

Aristotelian conception of the common good by positing that God is the

overall common good

(Aquinas, 1950). Rourke (1996) argued that the common good could be
categorized into

"formal and material parts" (p. 233). A formal part of the common good is a

quality term that does not reduce when split and dispersed among many and

can thus be shared, such as friendship, communion, citizenship, harmony,

peace, integrity, compassion, etc. A material part of the common good is a

quantitative term in which the efficacy of the good depends on whether it is

divided and distributed. It will diminish once divided. It can also be replaced

with the same quantity of the same good, such as natural resources, products,

and services.

The Catholic Perspective of the Common Good of Business

The Catholic perspective of the common good is commonly known as

originating from the Catholic Social Teachings (CST) (Catholic Church,

2000; Paul VI, 1967; Benedict XVI, 2009). Papal encyclicals, episcopal

pastoral letters, conciliar publications, and other official church teaching

documents are the authoritative sources of CST

(McCann, 2011; McVea & Naughton, 2021; Sison & Fontrodona, 2011,
2012, 2013).

Caritas in Veritate (CV) by Benedict XVI (2009) offered the latest characterization of the common good as "a good that is linked to living in society," that is, "the good of 'all of us,' made up of individuals, families and intermediate groups who together constitute society" (p.7).

Most literature attends to how business, as a separate subject, contributes to the common good of humanity (Mele, 2009; Moore, 2005; Mortreuil, 2009; O'Brien, 2009; T. W. Smith, 1999; Solomon, 1992, 2004; Wong & Rae, 2011). Sison and Fontrodona (2011, 2012, 2013), McVea and Naughton (2021), McCann (2011), and Faldetta (2012) worked on the common good of business itself to establish a theoretical and integral framework for discerning the purpose of business. Sison and Fontrodona (2011, 2012, 2013) reflected on the common good of business itself through the engagement of the encounter for an innovative transformation of business postured by CV. They discussed the conception of the common good of business and propose a methodology that presents principal characteristics of work rather than profit. They summarized the concerns and risks in terms of economic development brought forward by the CV: Economic activity is not only an integral part of human development but also "not inherently inhuman and opposed to society" (Benedict XVI, 2009, p. 36). Even though the short-term view might enhance financial profits, there are risks in the loss of long-term benefits for humanity. "Short-term economy—sometimes very short-term approach—needs to be carefully evaluated" (Benedict XVI, 2009, p.

32). Profit serves as a means rather than an end in the realm of business endeavors. The references provided in the text are CV 21, 70, and 71. Organizational responsibility extends beyond the interests of shareholders to encompass the concerns of stakeholders as well (CV 40). The logic of gratuitousness supersedes the logic of the exchange (CV 38).

Sison and Fontrodona (2011) asserted that the common good of business contributes to human growth just as the common good aids in defining the goals of a specific society. With these concerns, CST stipulates two definitions of the common good. One was "the sum total of social conditions which allow people, either as groups or as individuals, to reach their fulfillment more fully and more easily" (Catholic Church, 2000, para 1924). The other was the "development of the whole man and all men" (Paul VI, 1967, para. 42). These two definitions correspond with the material and formal parts of the common good, respectively, categorized by Rourke (1996).

> Drawing definition and inspiration of the common good of business from CV and

CST, McVea and Naughton (2021) focused their studies on "the total of social conditions" (p. 6). They argued that when functioning well, a business generates "three interdependent sets of goods" that furnish affluent dimensions to the common good of business: "good goods, good work, and good wealth." When all three of these outcomes are achieved, "businesses contribute positively to the common good by creating social conditions that increase the probability people will develop" (McVea & Naughton, 2021, p. 7).

According to McVea and Naughton (2021), the concept of Good Goods refers to a business that produces goods and services that effectively fulfill the global demands and requirements (p. 7); the concept also encompasses the idea that a good business demonstrates solidarity with marginalized and disadvantaged groups by actively seeking out opportunities to provide services to those who are typically overlooked or lacking in resources (p. 9). The concept of Good Work entails the notion that a business that is considered good is one that actively contributes to the community by promoting the dignity of human work and acknowledging its subjective dimension (p. 9). The concept of Good Wealth posits that the distribution of wealth is contingent upon its produce, and that sustainable wealth growth necessitates equitable distribution among its growers (p. 12).

In a similar vein, McVea and Naughton (2021) argued in favor of the principles of
"good goods, good work, and good wealth" as a potential foundation for all businesses. The flourishment of employees within a firm is contingent upon their ability to meet the demands of external stakeholders by providing high-quality products and services, as well as generating and distributing wealth (McVea & Naughton, 2021). However, McVea and
Naughton's framework pays limited attention to the local community and natural environmental in which the firm operates.

As a formal part of the common good from the same theme in Pope Benedict XVI's encyclical *Caritas in Veritate*, McCann (2011) and Faldetta (2012) concentrated their reflection on the logic of gratuitousness for social entrepreneurship. They introduced the concept of social capital in their studies in contrast to the logic of exchange (the commercial logic or the contractual logic) for solely-for-profit organizations with capital solely for financial means. According to Faldetta (2012), the logic of gratuitousness in business acts as a flow of products as an operational mechanism for creating connections with morally upstanding substance. He offered the logic of gratuitousness as "an alternative model for business and the social sciences to the logic of exchange (market) and the logic of public obligation (state) for the sake of an equilibrium between the market and the State" (p. 67). In the logic of gratuitousness, "we give because we have received," while in the logic of exchange, "we give in order to acquire," and in the logic of public obligation, "we give through duty" (p. 67). McCann (2011) reflected on the opportunities and challenges for business with the logic of gratuitousness by introducing the concept of "social capital" to "civilize the economy" by addressing social problems on a commercial basis (p. 1). He advocated that social capital can be generated by institutionalizing the principle of gratuitousness. It can be liberated by cultivating gratuitousness in all areas of society, including business.

The Catholic perspective of the common good of business is based on CV and CST. I shall review the literature in the following section based on the protestant perspectives of the common good of business.

Protestant Perspectives of the Common Good of Business

From a Protestant perspective, the Scripture is the source of authority (van den Belt, 2008). The Bible addresses the common good. Jesus says God "causes his sun to rise on the evil and the good and sends rain on the righteous and the unrighteous" (New International Version Bible, 2011/1973, Matthew 5:45). The common good is common to the good and the evil, the righteous and the unrighteous, i.e., common to all. The Bible explicitly spells out the word "common good" in 1 Corinthains 12:7 (New International Version Bible, 2011/1973). According to the Apostle Paul's teaching in 1 Corinthians 12, the common good is the good of "the same Spirit, the same Lord, and the same God" (New International Version Bible, 2011/1973, 1 Corinthians 12:4–7), i.e., the Trinitarian God, a God inherently relational from before the beginning of time. All the mighty acts of creation pour out of that connection. Since creation was deliberated to generate glory for God, the work of creation originated from the relationship that was anticipated to bring glory to the

Trinity.

Emil Brunner emphasized the relationality evident in 1 Corinthians 12 in the Bible as central to the image of God as a representative function of the image—its relational dynamic. Accordingly, we are called to live in the right and responsible relationships with God, other human beings, and nature

(Plantinga et al., 2010). Abraham Kuyper extended

Emil Brunner's notion of the centrality of relationality in the common good

by discussing the ideas of "sphere sovereignty" (Hexham, 1983). He defined

five spheres: "the church, education, the family, the state, and society" (p. 4).

As Turnbull (2018) pointed out, Kuyper's idea of sphere sovereignty is

principally responsible for the common good of the society with "its

powerful expressions of localism" (p. 19). He stated, "Although the role of

the state cannot be excluded, it is, however, limited" (p. 17). Kuyper's

concept of sphere sovereignty helps hold each sphere to its sovereign role

with its own privileges and duties, and its own obligations in promoting the

common good, not just the state alone. In his analysis, Van Duzer (2010)

aligned himself with Wolterstorff (1983) in critiquing the notion that specific

institutions had inherent, unchanging ontological roles as bestowed by God.

The authors contended that it is preferable for various domains of social

function to be integrated in a complimentary manner, rather than being

segregated with distinct advantages, responsibilities, and obligations.

According to Vorster (2016), in John Calvin's view, the natural laws of

the common good originated from God's very nature with his sovereignty,

magnificence, and his providence and purpose. "God expressed his common

goodness to all people by giving them creational gifts. The fact that

humankind was created in the image of God is an affirmation of the

remarkable gifts that God has bestowed on all people" (p. 2). As a metaphor from John Wesley, humanity as the image of God is like a triangular prism that reflects what we receive from God and refracts into the world. Therefore, the image is not something humanity has or is lodged within the human being but is an ongoing relationship in which humanity receives and gives. What is received is love, which is then reflected to

God and outward to God's offspring, who likewise bear the image of their Creator. (Lodahl

& Powell, 2012, p. 80)

Consistent with John Calvin and John Wesley, Adam Smith discovered a harmonious order in nature as a part of natural theology. The mechanisms of economic equilibrium function through this order for the common good (A. Smith & Wight, 2007).

Adam Smith (1812) defined "the essential concepts of a market economic model, i.e., value, price, cost, and exchange, and advocated a minimalist approach to government intervention in the workings of the market" (A. Smith, 1812, as cited in Turnbull, 2018, p. 12). The economic mechanism's effect is to produce common welfare for everyone by pursuing their interests. Smith argued that a greater communal good could be achieved in this way. Smith claimed:

The principles of natural compassion are Implanted in man, and the paradox in the classical business model between the pursuit of self-interest on the part of individuals and the overall achievement of the public good could be explained by the providential design of those laws of economics, which brought this about. (A. Smith, 1812, as cited in Turnbull, 2018, p. 13)

This "natural theology" associates the market economy with Protestants. It is worth noting that natural theology is not a synthetic theory but a reflection of God's providence in the stewardship of His creation. The common good is economical and humane in God's image.

Thomas Chalmers continued with Calvinism and Smithian economics in exploring the natural law of economic equilibrium (Hilton, 2001). In the second volume of his *Natural Theology*, Chalmers (1836) discerned how the natural law influenced the society's economic and political well-being with an outcome he called the law of relative affection (i.e., individuals acting in their own interests) or, afterward, back to the paradox of selfinterest resulting to the common good. Following Smith's natural theology, the law of relative affection hypothesizes the individual consideration for the concern and deprivation of others as a natural seed implanted in humanity (Chalmers, 1836, as cited in Turnbull, 2018). Chalmers (1836) claimed that "the philosophy of free trade is grounded on principle, that society is most enriched or best served when commerce is left to its own spontaneous evolution" (Chalmers, 1836, as cited in Turnbull, 2018, pp. 136–137). He believed that the most significant economic good (the common good of business) is positively associated with the freedom of a market system. However, Chalmers' natural theology was not meant for human beings not to do anything and for God to handle everything but to pursue a rigorous and restricted goal with individual interests in one's own sphere of sovereignty.

On God's sovereignty, "the markets are best supplied" (Chalmers, 1836, as cited in

Turnbull, 2018, p. 137).

In contrast, Van Duzer (2010), with an evangelical Presbyterian tradition, reached the conclusion, following a comprehensive analysis of the market economy and the Garden economy (the Garden of Eden), that Adam Smith's concept of the "invisible hand" cannot be attributed to divine intervention (p.76). A market economy is predicated on the concept of scarcity, whereas a Garden economy is distinguished by its state of abundance. In a market economy, individuals are expected to act in their own self-interests, with their influence determined by their financial resources. Conversely, a Garden economy is centered around the collective welfare, prioritizing the common good. In the market economy, an individual's worth is assessed based on their productive contributions, as livelihood is earned. On the other hand, the Garden economy places emphasis on the inherent blessings bestowed by God. God engages in the act of bestowing upon individuals that which they have not earned. The concept of divine value is rooted in the belief that every human is regarded by God as a cherished child, created in His likeness, and deserving of the benevolent offerings bestowed by God (Van Duzer, 2010).

Following a careful examination of the Catholic perspective on the common good as outlined in CST, specifically pertaining to human rights, human development, and community development, Van Duzer (2010), posited that the primary objective of business at its fundamental level is to provide goods and services, as well as generate opportunities for individuals. This objective, referred to as the "first-order" purpose of business (p.43), is distinct from the secondary goals of fostering relationships and promoting communitybuilding. According to Van Duzer, in the Genesis narrative, Adam and Eve collaborate with God in order to facilitate the cultivation of the land, resulting in the production of crops that serve to sustain the material welfare of both humanity and the broader natural world. Adam and Eve, via the execution of these responsibilities, contribute to the advancement of God's mission and consequently bestow honor upon Him. These activities, when performed collectively, contribute to the flourishing of the society in accordance with the divine plan, and can thus be referred to as Genesis activities. These actions are to be pursued for the glory of God and, as it is occasionally expressed, "for the common good" (p.39). Van Duzer posited that it is imperative for every Christian involved in business to actively participate in all the Genesis activities. Consequently, Van Duzer argued that business serves as an institution for generating wealth and facilitating structured avenues for purposeful labor, so enabling employees to manifest their innate creativity bestowed upon them by God. Therefore, apart from its instrumental value of generating wealth, the objective of business also possesses an intrinsic value in facilitating avenues for individuals inside the organization to manifest their calling through the execution of labor that brings glory to God. When managers actively pursue these specific objectives for their organizations, they are directly engaging in the fulfillment of God's creation mandate and contributing to the promotion of the common good (Van Duzer, 2010).

In summary, the Bible defines the common good as the Triune God's good for all (New International Version Bible, 2011/1973, Matthew 5:45, 1 Corinthians 12:4–7). A healthy relationship with God, others, and nature is the common good (Plantinga et al.,

2010). Kuyper claimed that "sphere sovereignty" and the common good are not the state's exclusive concerns, expanding Emil Brunner's idea of the common good's primacy, limited state (Hexham, 1983). However, Wolterstorff (1983) and Van Duzer (2010) argued that complementary integrated social functioning is preferable to dividing it with separate advantages, responsibilities, and obligations. Calvin believed that God's sovereignty, majesty, providence, and purpose created the natural rules of the common good (Vorster, 2016). Smith discovered some of the natural laws of economics as mechanisms of economic equilibrium through the market (A. Smith, 1812, as cited in Turnbull, 2018, p. 12); Chalmers (1836) continued the Smithian concept with the law of relative affection of self-interest resulting in the common good. Van Duzer (2010) disagreed, arguing that Adam Smith's "invisible hand" is not divine intervention (p.76). Van Duzer (2010) emphasized that business's intrinsic purpose is human flourishing via employment, and its instrumental purpose is wealth generation through the production of goods and services for the common good.

While the Catholic viewpoint derives its authority from the Canon of Scripture and the teachings of the Church, protestant perspectives are rooted only in the Scriptures. It is important to note that despite their differing sources of authority, both the Catholic and Protestant perspectives are grounded in the Christian faith. I intended to conduct a comprehensive examination of the scholarly literature pertaining to the concept of the common good within the realm of business, employing a scientific approach.

A Scientific Perspective of the Common Good of Business

As gratitude is considered a formal part of the common good, is there any evidencebased research and practices of gratitude in educational, medical, and organizational contexts for the common good? In collaboration with Robert Emmons of the University of California at Davis, the Greater Good Science Center of the University of California at Berkeley launched the Expanding the Science and Practice of Gratitude research project in 2011 (Allen, 2018). It was a multi-year project to develop the scientific database of gratitude, especially in critical human health, personal and relational welfare, and developmental science. In May 2018, the center published a white paper named "The Science of Gratitude" (Allen, 2018).

According to Algoe and Way (2014), their research has revealed that neuroscience has identified certain brain regions that are closely associated with the emotion and expression of gratitude. This finding provides more support for the notion that gratitude is an intrinsic element of the human experience. Numerous scholarly investigations have additionally discerned specific genetic factors that might play a role in the manifestation of gratitude in individuals (Allen, 2018). The emergence of gratitude is witnessed in children as they advance through their initial phases of maturation and development (Allen, 2018).

The concept of gratitude is influenced by both inherent predispositions and external factors. The correlation between employee personality and organizational culture is evident. Dispositional gratitude has been found to be connected with specific personality qualities, namely extraversion, agreeableness, conscientiousness, neuroticism, and experienceseeking (C.-C. Lin, 2015; Liu et al., 2017). There are several distinct qualities, namely envy, materialism, narcissism, and cynicism, that serve as impediments to the expression of gratitude. The presence of these hurdles has the potential to have a detrimental impact on the operational productivity of a firm, as suggested by previous research conducted by Solom et al. (2017) and Tsang et al. (2014). In a study conducted by Lambert et al. (2009), those who were designated to engage in prayers for their mate or engage in general prayer over a period of four weeks had a higher level of gratitude compared to those who were instructed to contemplate their daily activities. This study implied a potential correlation between spirituality and dispositional gratitude. The inclusion of gratitude within the framework of the common good in business signifies that the amalgamation of Christian faith and business administration encompasses both theological and scientific dimensions. According to Allen (2018), gratitude is associated with various advantages for individuals, such as improved physical and psychological well-being, heightened pleasure and life satisfaction, reduced materialism, and other positive outcomes. Organizational behavior is a field of research within psychology that places considerable emphasis on the physical and psychological well-being of individuals. The physical and psychological well-being of business stakeholders, particularly employees, has a direct association with corporate productivity, regardless of whether the organization is for-profit or non-profit. According to Morgan et al. (2017), gratitude has been recognized as "the mother of all virtues" due to its potential to facilitate the development of various other virtues, such as patience, humility, and wisdom. According to Krumrei-Mancuso (2017), virtues such as patience, humility, discipline, wisdom, creativity, diversity, and respect have the potential to be regarded as valuable assets for a firm. Gratitude serves as a driving force for individuals to exhibit increased levels of compassion, kindness, and prosocial behavior. Additionally, it plays a pivotal role in fostering stronger interpersonal relationships, including romantic relationships. Furthermore, gratitude has the potential to enhance the overall atmosphere within a professional setting (A. M. Grant & Gino, 2010). The prosocial strength of a team inside a firm is closely linked to marketing, sales, and customer services. According to Allen (2018), expressing gratitude has the potential to enhance employees' job performance, increase their job satisfaction, and promote prosocial behaviors such as helpfulness and respect towards their colleagues. The level of employee satisfaction is a crucial determinant of business productivity.

In summary, gratitude, as an integral component of the common good, has a direct or indirect impact on the physical and psychological well-being of individuals. This influence is mediated by an internal cognitive framework and serves as a cohesive force in fostering relationships among stakeholders of the business, so strengthening the foundation of the community.

Summary of the Common Good of Business

From a biological science point of view, gratitude is both nature and nurture. From a philosophical understanding, gratitude is a formal part of the common good. From the Catholic perspective, the common good of business is expressed as "good goods, good work, and good wealth" (McVea & Naughton, 2021, p. 15). From the protestant perspectives, the common good of business is common and good to all people through human dignity and respect for the market toward the Garden business. The intrinsic purpose of a business is to facilitate human flourishing by means of providing employment opportunities, while its instrumental purpose is to generate wealth via the production of goods and services that contribute to the common good. Limited knowledge is about how the stakeholders of rural Midwestern American businesses perceive their purposes for business. Through the Catholic, protestants, and scientific influences given within the setting of my research, I intended to comprehend their perceptions of the common good for business.

Business Model

In the preceding sections, many viewpoints of the common good of business, sometimes referred to as the aim of business, were examined. The operational aspects of a business, ranging from its underlying purpose to the diverse methods of implementation, are contingent upon its internal framework, known as the business model. As stated by Massa et al. (2017), the business model of a profit-making entity can be defined as a comprehensive depiction of the organization and its operational mechanisms for attaining its objectives within several domains such as economic, social, spiritual, ecological, cultural, and others (p. 1). The design of a business model primarily encompasses the fundamental elements of purpose, structure, and process (Geissdoerfer et al., 2017).

The Common Good of Business Models

The intrinsic values of business, as discussed in the preceding section, can be traced back to their divine origins in God. The bestowal of divine benevolence is seen in the endowment of individuals with entrepreneurial aptitude, manifesting as discernment and innovative concepts for the purpose of engaging in business. Novak (1990) posited in his publication titled *Toward a Theology of the Corporation* that the principal capital of a firm are comprised of human creativity, knowledge, and ideas. The engine serves as a catalyst and facilitates the exploration of the Creator's valuable assets within the realm of business. The major resource of any firm is derived from the insights provided by individuals. The possession of wealth in and of itself does not automatically qualify as capital. The transformation of a tangible asset into capital is contingent upon the presence of insightful understanding. Hence, human knowledge stands as the primary manifestation of riches. An individual who holds a substantial amount of casino chips and engages in gambling activities cannot be classified as a capitalist. The individual possessing valuable knowledge transforms into a capitalist. According to Novak (1990), the presence of insight has a significant impact (p. 42). In contrast, Novak provided an illustration of a socialist perspective, wherein Karl Marx erroneously posited that capital essentially pertains to tangible means of production, such as machinery, money, and other fixed or current assets. Marx neglected to acknowledge the extent to which "the primary form of capital is an idea"

(p. 41).

The tentmaking enterprise, as shown in the biblical Book of Acts, highlights the bestowal of entrepreneurial acumen upon Priscilla and Aquila by God, as well as the acquisition of tentmaking expertise by Aquila and the Apostle Paul throughout their youth.

In a gratuitous manner, it can be observed that Priscilla and Aquila were providentially equipped by God with their respective entrepreneurial acumen and abilities, which served as a foundation for their collaborative and economically viable tentmaking enterprise. This providential encounter occurred at a certain juncture in their lives. Therefore, the capital required to operate a business is determined by the combination of intangible knowledge and tangible resources in the form of equity. The aforementioned capital is subsequently utilized to generate financial gains by means of producing goods and delivering services, as depicted Figure 1.

The Shareholder Wealth Maximization Model

Today, a prevailing business model taught in most business schools is the Shareholder-Wealth-Maximization (SWM) model. The SWM model stipulates that a forprofit business's-direct functional objective and explicit purpose should be to maximize equity capital returns (Jensen & Meckling, 1976; Windsor, 2010). Under the SWM model, determining which product or service a business could produce or offer should constitute the basis for evaluating which products or services would generate the maximum profit for shareholders of the business. Windsor (2010) argued that the SWM model's operational objective is theoretically to generate "the most socially effective capital allocation" (p.437). Mainstream economists argued that the management of the business has a moral responsibility to operate the business in every means to maximize the company's profit (Friedman, 2007; Sundaram & Inkpen, 2004).

Sison and Fontrodona (2011) argued that the SWM model exploits the paradox of

"self-interest resulting in the common good" in the context of economic freedom for the growth of productivity by assuming the compartmentalization of the material part (i.e., food, water, machine, profit, asset, equity, and capital) from the formal part (i.e., the relationships of God-human, human-human, and human-nature such as knowledge, friendship, citizenship, solidarity, peace, justice, and charity) of the common good. The SWM model, according to Mcleod (2024), separates people's physiological needs from their desires for security, a sense of belonging, respect, and self-actualization. Some questions could be asked, "Is a business model related to the development stage of a particular economic system? Can a for-profit organization have the sole responsibility of the material part of its stakeholders' common good or physiological needs?" Van Duzer (2010) asserted that, in this model, investing in ingenious employee relationships and serving the contractors, consumers, and suppliers with gratuitousness are decent operational strategies "to the extent, and only to the extent" that they increase the bottom line of the operating profit. By explanation, corporate relationships with stakeholders are converted to a means for maximizing shareholders' wealth (p. 46).

According to Yahanpath and Joseph (2011), while analyzing the case studies surrounding the global financial crisis of 2007–2009, it may be stated that the primary factors leading to this disaster were an abundance of greed and an unwavering focus on SWM. The case studies conducted by Yahanpath and Joseph (2011) shed light on some detrimental consequences associated with the SWM business model. These included instances of unethical behavior, challenges related to agency conflicts, executive compensation packages, manipulative accounting practices, and the transfer of risks.

According to the SWM model, it is posited that a for-profit entity bears exclusive accountability for the material part of the common good, specifically the financial requirements of its stakeholders. Therefore, the SWM model prioritizes the maximization of profits for the benefit of shareholder wealth, whether it pertains to the business's assets or the personal wealth accumulation of the shareholders. This is demonstrated in Figure 2.

The Stakeholder Theory Model

The term "stakeholder" was initially employed by the Stanford Research Institute in the year 1963 (Freeman & Reed, 1983). Ever since the release of Freeman's highly influential paper titled *"Strategic Management: A Stakeholder Approach"* in 1984 (Freeman, 1984), an alternative perspective on comprehending the role of management has emerged, commonly referred to as stakeholder theory. The contemporary stakeholder theory posits that management has obligations towards both shareholders and other constituent groups who possess a vested interest in the organization. These groups include employees, suppliers, local communities, creditors, society with a focus on social responsibility, and the environment with an emphasis on ecological responsibility (T. C. W. Lin, 2018). This concept is illustrated in Figure 3, which can be found in the figure. The ST model posits that social responsibility is characterized by a moral stance that prioritizes the common good of the business. The application of the law of moral sentiments to the flourishing of stakeholders is observed alongside the law of self-preservation (Turnbull, 2018).

Adam Smith formulated the law of moral sentiments as a theory of ethics in his work titled "The Theory of Moral Sentiments," published in 1759. Smith posited that moral judgments derive from our inherent ability to empathize with others. The capacity in question was referred to as the "moral sense" (A. Smith, 2002). Smith posited that moral judgments are formed through the process of empathetically placing oneself in the perspective of the individuals implicated in a given scenario. Subsequently, we contemplate our emotional state if we were to assume their circumstances. If individuals elicit sympathy, it is indicative of our positive evaluation of their conduct. If individuals do not experience sympathy for others, they tend to evaluate their actions as morally negative. Smith further posited that individuals do not merely assume a passive role as mere spectators of their own moral judgments. Additionally, there exists a human inclination to seek validation and approval from one's peers. The aforementioned inclination serves as the impetus for individuals to engage in behaviors that align with ethical standards (A. Smith, 2009).

The law of self-preservation pertains to an individual or a state's entitlement to undertake requisite measures to safeguard itself from potential harm or danger. The innate need to evade danger and ensure one's survival is a fundamental aspect of human nature. The aforementioned principle holds significant importance in the fields of biology and psychology, and its influence is also evident in the domains of law and ethics (Martinich, 2021). Within the realm of ethics, the law of self-preservation is frequently invoked to rationalize behaviors that have the potential to do harm to others, however, under the condition that the harm inflicted upon oneself would be more substantial. The consumption of meat is commonly regarded as ethically permissible despite its inherent involvement in the act of animal death due to the fundamental necessity of sustenance for human survival (Frowe & Parry, 2022).

The underlying principle of this approach is to achieve a harmonious equilibrium between economic expansion and societal responsibility, while adopting a business strategy that encompasses not only shareholder profit but also broader societal benefits. According to Phillips et al. (2019), the ST model commonly employs market-based and resourcebased business strategies at the socio-political level.

A market-based business strategy is a strategic approach that prioritizes the fulfillment of consumer demands within a specific market segment. This particular approach is grounded in the notion that enterprises might achieve success by comprehending and addressing the demands of their clientele (Dawar, 2013). A resourcebased business strategy pertains to a strategic approach wherein a company capitalizes on its distinct resources and competencies in order to attain a competitive edge. This particular approach is grounded in the notion that enterprises can achieve success by discerning and capitalizing on their distinctive capabilities (R. M. Grant, 1991).

To better understand the organizational behaviors under the ST model, Donaldson and Preston (1995) proposed to detail the ST model into three interrelated directives, i.e., the descriptive ST, normative ST, and instrumental ST. The descriptive ST empirically describes how corporate executives and other stakeholders behave. The normative ST explains how corporate executives and other stakeholders should behave. The instrumental ST provides the theoretical connections between stakeholder management practices and the corporate operational outcome. Although the normative perspective should be the core of the ST, the instrumental motivation could be for the firm to fulfill social obligation strategically to maximize shareholders' profit. Applying both laws of self-preservation and the law of moral sentiments is thus incomplete (Turnbull, 2018).

The Common Good Model

The SWM model places its primary emphasis on the accumulation of capital for the benefit of shareholders, while the ST model highlights the social responsibilities of the firm. In response to these prevailing models, scholars have introduced an alternative framework known as the Common Good (CG) model (Felber, 2019; McVea & Naughton,

2021; Rieger, 2015; Rourke, 1996; Sison & Fontrodona, 2011, 2013; Turnbull, 2018; Van

Duzer, 2010; Wong & Rae, 2011). Despite the existence of numerous suggestions about the CG model, a common thread among them is the shift from prioritizing profit as the primary objective of a corporation under the

SWM model to considering profit as a means to an end and placing the common good as the ultimate purpose of business.

Felber (2019) offered a proposal called The Economy for the Common Good model with three fundamental building blocks, i.e., human dignity, sustainability, and democracy, to reconcile the broken relationships between the economy and feelings, the economy and democracy, and between the economy and nature. For practitioners and scholars, Felber developed a tool called the common good balance sheet. "The common good balance sheet measures to which degree a company lifts and promotes constitutional values from human dignity over sustainability to democracy" (Felber, 2019, p. 22). He claimed that the common good balance sheet is meant to be a visible hand that makes the dream of Adam Smith come true. It results in private enterprises and free markets that cause the common good. In this balance sheet, a company's ethical performance and constitutional fidelity will be visible. All products and services will tell consumers transparently who made them, under which conditions, and with which ecological impact. If the firm is solidarity, if it pays a fair tax or hides profits in tax havens, consumers will have a better informed and freer choice. The innovation of the common good balance sheet is to reconcile the disassociation between prices and business ethics. Currently, the more ethical products are more expensive on the market, while less ethical products enjoy a competitive advantage for being cheaper. In an ethical market economy, it should be the other way around. They link the common good balance sheet results in a differentiated legal treatment from taxes over tariffs and loan conditions. Consequently, the ethical products and services will become cheaper to consumers than the less ethical ones, and only responsible competitors will remain in the market. The renowned laws of the market would be in coherence with the values of the common good (Felber, 2019).

In an empirical study, Felber et al. (2019) used a sample of 206 out of a population of 400 firms in Europe. As of December 31, 2017, these firms have produced and audited the common good balance sheet employing the economy for the common good model to evaluate the interactions of the businesses with their stakeholders in terms of corporate sustainability by using the common good matrix and the common good balance sheet as the tools (Felber, 2019; Frémeaux & Michelson, 2017). The purpose of the empirical study was to illustrate the business strategies that the economy for the common good model uses. The common good matrix and the common good balance sheet were validated as a tool to measure the performance outcome of a firm that employed the economy for the common good model. A system known as integrated reporting was used to assess an organization's performance regarding its effects on the social and ecological spheres. This system was created and adopted by various businesses worldwide (Felber et al., 2019).

Derived from the Catholic Social Teachings (CST) and the *Caritas in Veritate* (CV), McCann (2011) and Faldetta (2012) introduced another proposal for the CG model with the law of gratitude in the business relationship. Sison and Fontrodona (2011) laid down a foundation of the common good of business with a distinction of material and formal parts of the common good. They further categorized the profit as a material part and the work as a formal part of the common good. Building on the framework of material and formal parts of the common good, McVea and Naughton (2021) advanced three principles,

i.e., "good goods, good work, and good wealth" (p. 1). These three principles are strategic building blocks of the CG model, where the essential elements of good goods are to "meet the needs of the world and solidarity with the poor" (McVea & Naughton, 2021, p. 7). The dimensions of the good work are "dignity of work and subsidiarity" (McVea & Naughton,

2021, p. 12). The extents of good wealth are "wealth creation and just distribution" (McVea & Naughton, 2021, p. 15). McVea and Naughton (2021) provided examples of "good goods" suppliers of Cargill, Kraft, General Mills, Monsanto, Pillsbury, Supervalue, and Target who "have enabled the poor and the hungry to spend a smaller percentage of their income on food" (p.7); as an example of "good work," Mohammad Yunus, the recipient of the Nobel Peace Prize and a founding member of the for-profit Grameen Bank provided microloans for women and helped millions of people escape poverty. Despite being a forprofit organization, his work has made him stand out as one of the greatest moral role models of good work. In their paper, McVea and Naughton (2021) presented an opposite example of "good wealth" where Andrew Carnegie paid millions of dollars to compensate the damage caused by the pollution produced by his factory, and the relationships among the business stakeholders were debilitated (p.13).

From protestant perspectives, Van Duzer (2010), Chalmers (2010), and Turnbull (2018) began with the law of gratitude for the reconciliation of broken relationships between God and humanity, among human beings, and between humanity and nature. They believed that the root causes of the non-sustainability in business today are the consequences of these broken relationships. To restore a good God-human relationship, businesspeople need to turn their worship from wealth to God with their ultimate faith and attach securely to God without fearing anything else but God. Entrepreneurs also need to place their basic human needs in the providence of God, account for the human intelligence of all stakeholders as a capital of the company, and install their physical, emotional, relational, and spiritual rest in God (Tan, 2003). To restore the good relationships among the business stakeholders, they want to experience the servanthood of Christ Jesus (Tan, 2006) and practice neighbor economics (Nelson, 2017). Business owners also want to treat stakeholders with dignity due to those made in God's image and replace hierarchy and dominance with the mode of cooperation in the workplace (Van Duzer, 2010). To reestablish a good relationship between humanity and nature with the fulfillment of the creation mandate, business stakeholders need to be aware of the consequences of the disrupted harmony of the entire created order. All participants of the business ought to conceptualize the restoration of the human-nature relation as a social obligation and a reflection of God's grace for the greater glory of God and shift the account of such effort from expense to investment. The "purpose for people, prosperity, and the planet" is a call to "live simple" and "reduce the carbon footprint" (Stolze, 2021, p. 152).

From a scientific standpoint, the Creator's design of a comprehensive and flawless atmospheric system necessitates the incorporation of three essential characteristics: reception, refraction, and reflection. These features are crucial in achieving the ultimate equilibrium of sunlight distribution, thereby ensuring the long-term sustainability of both the atmosphere and the planet Earth. The accumulation of energy within the atmosphere may have adverse effects on both the atmosphere and the Earth. Excessive retention of solar energy on the Earth's surface could lead to the phenomenon of global warming. The current climate is undergoing transformation in the following manner. The principles of physics govern the amount of energy that must be reflected back to the sun by both the Earth and the atmosphere (University of California Museum of Paleontology, n.d.).

In order to achieve sustainable development, it is argued that businesses should possess three essential characteristics: reception, refraction, and reflection. These attributes enable businesses to attain a state of equilibrium in the distribution of divine endowments, such as insights and wealth, for the betterment of society and the preservation of the natural world. The CG model adheres to the laws of self-preservation, moral sentiments, and gratitude, respectively, as depicted in Figure 4.

According to the CG model, the determination of which product or service to make or deliver is contingent upon evaluating which option would optimize the creation sustainability for the common good. Considering the inherent capabilities and resources of the organization, the managerial personnel of the CG enterprise ought to strategize the optimal allocation of resources in order to effectively provide goods and services. This approach will facilitate the flourishing and sustainability of the community, fostering harmonious relationships between God and humanity, among individuals, and between humanity and nature.

Summary of Business Model

The field of business is intricately connected to the realm of employment. Human beings are meant to be created as co-workers of God, engaging in the act of creation in a manner that reflects the likeness of God. Hence, business models incorporate the concept of the common good in conjunction with the utilization of God's bestowed gifts to humanity. The possession of creative ideas and insightful perspectives serves as a fundamental resource for all firms, regardless of their specific business strategies.

The widely adopted SWM model has been taught in business schools and practiced by businesses in the world such as publicly traded corporations as "a standard assumption" (Windsor, 2010, p. 437). Under the SWM model, the corporate financial outcome dominates the organizational performance measurement as a single bottom-line approach. Most profit is channeled to shareholder wealth which may contribute to the material part of the common good depending on the shareholders' free will. Other stakeholders of the business have much less influence on wealth distribution. Social and environmental aspects of the business are not accounted for as corporate sustainability concerns simply because they are non-financials (Felber et al., 2019).

With corporate sustainability concerns, the ST model was introduced utilizing a triple-bottom-line strategy, i.e., financial, social, and ecological, with stakeholders being the core of the sustainable corporate strategy rather than shareholders. The creation of an integrated reporting system could evaluate stakeholder opinions and enables their involvement in the process to guarantee that corporate sustainability management is practiced with social and ecological concerns (Felber et al., 2019).

In a proposed CG model from Felber et al. (2019), called the economy for the common good model, the common good matrix and the common good balance sheet were introduced for businesses to assess and report the ethical and human values (social justice, human dignity, and solidarity, co-determination, transparency, and environmental sustainability), and to evaluate the degree of relationship between the business activities the for-profit organization engages in with its various stakeholders (employees, owners, customers, suppliers, and service providers). Human rights are considered the common good under the faith-neutral the economy for the common good paradigm (Felber, 2019). Another proposal of the CG model from McVea and Naughton (2021) was based on the three constructs of "good goods, good work, and good wealth" (p.4). For faith-based forprofit organizations, the spiritual dimension was introduced as the fourth bottom line in addition to the triple-bottom-line approach (Chalmers, 2010; Nelson, 2017; Tan, 2006; Turnbull, 2018; Van Duzer, 2010). Under this proposal, restoration and reconciliation of the relationships of God-human, human-human, and human-nature were placed in the core of the spiritual dimension of the CG model. Resources of a faith-based for-profit organization should be optimally distributed in all four dimensions, spiritual, financial, social, and ecological, as a quadruple bottom-line approach for corporate sustainability strategy and reporting system. The primary constructs of SWM, ST, and CG business models are summarized in Table 1.

Business as Ministry

In the tentmaking testimony reported in Chapter 18 of the Book of Acts in the Bible, the Apostle Paul first exemplified business as ministry (N. Johnson & Rundle, 2006). During his second missionary journey, the Apostle Paul made friends with Priscilla and Aquila, a Jewish couple at Corinth who had recently arrived from Rome, where they had been forced to flee (New International Version Bible, 2011/1973, Acts 18:1–2). Priscilla and Aquila were tentmakers when Claudius Caesar banished Jews from the city (H. S. Martin, 2018). Every Jewish boy might have to master a talent for survival as he grew up. When Paul and Aquila were young, they were most likely taught how to make tents. They knew how to cut and stitch goat's hair woven material into tents. The tents were sold to the market (M. N. Keller, 2010). Acts 18:3 says that Priscilla and Aquila welcomed Paul to reside and work in their home. While they were tentmakers, Paul used the business as a platform to thoroughly teach Priscilla and Aquila the Scripture (New International Version Bible, 2011/1973). Priscilla and Aquila became followers of Jesus Christ and Paul's particular disciples (M. N. Keller, 2010). This couple subsequently used their business to share their knowledge of God and their life experience in Christ with others as a Christian ministry (New International Version Bible, 2011/1973, Acts 18:4). Apollos, a

Jew, was a well-versed scholar of the Scriptures (Acts 18:24). Priscilla and Aquila brought

Apollos to their house and shared with him about Jesus Christ and the way to God through Him (H. S. Martin, 2018). Apollos accepted Christ as his personal savior and then traveled to the Corinthian region to help spread the gospel and serve the people there (New

International Version Bible, 2011/1973, Acts 18:27–28).

A Brief History of Business as Ministry Scholarship

> Contingent on the missionary example of the Apostle Paul with his co-workers

Priscilla and Aquila, missiologists and practitioners started to experiment to utilize lay

Christians' professional skills as a vehicle for God's mission. Around the mid-20th century, scholars began to use the word "tentmaking" to describe the role of business in the world mission (Rundle, 2012). The term "business as mission" was initially coined in 1999 by scholars at the Oxford Center for Mission Studies with a global mission strategy for the least reached and the least resourced in the world (N. Johnson & Rundle, 2006). In the mid20th century, tentmaking experimentalists Christy Wilson, Ken Crowell, and Ruth Seimens practiced the model in which "one's professional training and experience can be assets for world mission rather than liabilities" (Rundle, 2012, p. 67). In July 1989, during the Lausanne II Congress in Manila, the Lausanne Committee for World Evangelization issued the Lausanne Statement on Tentmaking (Lai, 2005). The Lausanne Statement established local churches with the duty to recruit and train persons for cross-cultural evangelism among unreached people groups. It also recognized the responsibility of church congregations in global missions (Nichols, 1989). In 2004, the Lausanne Committee for World Evangelization produced an official document, Lausanne Occasional Paper No. 59, which stated that "business is a mission, a calling, a ministry in its own right" (Tunehag et al., 2004, p. 12). It affirmed further that "ultimately churches, mission agencies, and kingdom businesses have the same purpose: to bring glory to God's name among all nations" (Tunehag et al., 2004, p. 48).

Various Forms of Business as Ministry

Different forms of business as ministry may have different evangelistic focus as a

Christian ministry. In their article, *Finishing the Task: The Unreached Peoples Challenge,* Winter and Koch (2002) introduced an evangelical measurement tool called "E-scale of evangelism." "E-0 evangelism" evangelizes "churchgoers" within one's own culture. "E-1 evangelism" refers to "near-neighbor evangelism." With E-1 evangelism, one crosses only one boundary from Christian to non-Christian groups, "between the church and the world." The culture and language persist the same. Language and cultural barriers are especially important in "E-2 evangelism," which requires breaching a second boundary (though not enormous). "E-3 evangelism" describes missions across even bigger boundaries and cultural differences to the "cultures very different from that of the messenger" (Winter & Koch, 2002, p. 17). Winter and Koch's E-scale can be used to categorize the following various forms of business as ministry.

Tentmaking

The definition of tentmaking was provided in a Lausanne Occasional Paper (Tunehag et al., 2004) as "tentmaking refers primarily to the practice of Christian professionals, who support themselves financially by working as employees or by engaging in business" (p. 13). Missionary professionals can carry out their ministries in tentmaking without burdening the people they serve or depending on donors. Tentmaking suggests combining work and testimony, emphasizing lay Christians' evangelism instead of the clergy or professional missionaries. Tentmaking can be applied to the contexts of E2 and

E3 evangelism in Winter and Koch's E-scale.

Marketplace Ministry

> A definition of marketplace ministry is given in the Lausanne Occasional Paper No.

59:

> Marketplace (workplace) ministries are principally focused on taking the Gospel to people where they work, mainly through the witness of co-workers and professional colleagues. These ministries encourage the integration of biblical principles into every aspect of business practice, to the glory of God. (Tunehag et al., p. 13)

Marketplace ministry organizations are broadly those as mission within the marketplace. They engage Christian businesspeople as business fellowships for "mutual support, evangelistic outreach, and workplace discipleship" (C. N. Johnson, 2009, p. 144).

Marketplace ministries can be applied to the contexts of E0 and E1 Evangelism in Winter's E-Scale (Winter & Koch, 2002).

Enterprise Development

Enterprise development can be "microenterprise development, small and medium enterprise development, or microfinance institutions or microloan programs" (C. N. Johnson, 2009, p. 144). They are devoted to the least reached and support the development of the least resourced communities through Christian non-profit organizations. They are also known internationally as non-governmental organizations (NGOs) "to help indigenous people improve their lives by starting and developing businesses" (C. N. Johnson, 2009, p.

144). Enterprise development can be applied to the context of E0 and E3 evangelism in

Winter's E-scale (Winter et al., 2013).

Business as Mission

The term *business as mission* was established in 1999 at the Oxford Center for Mission Studies to define a global Christian missional strategy of using business as a vehicle to reach the world's least-resourced and least-reached regions (N. Johnson & Rundle, 2006). It was initially an idea of missionaries going to the mission fields with a vehicle of business in a cross-cultural context. Missionaries are equipped with a passion for mission, skills of business, and sufficient initial capital to enter a least-reached or leastresourced cross-cultural mission field to start up a transnational for-profit business as a Christian mission. According to the business as mission document of the Lausanne Committee for World Evangelization (Tunehag et al., 2004), God established the institution and practice of business to carry out His creation mandate of stewardship over all creation. He is leveraging the power of business to help fulfill the Great Commission of making disciples of all peoples. God longs to be honored through human entrepreneur ventures.

Gort and Tunehag (2018) have a broader concept of business as mission in the context of the missiological paradigm-shifting for more lay Christians to pursue a manner of living the full embodied Gospel in their place of employment and daily life that is missional. It involves proclaiming and displaying the Kingdom of God in the marketplace everywhere. In this way, "God is always a stakeholder. He is the ultimate owner of our businesses. We want to see Christ manifested and God glorified through our businesses" (pp.169–170). Business as mission can be practiced in the context of E2 and E3 evangelism of Winter's E-scale (Winter et al., 2013). Various Forms of Business as Ministry are summarized in Table 2.

Empirical Studies of Business as Ministry

Most scholarly writing on business as ministry (or business as mission) focused on the perceptions of business owners and corporate leadership. C. M. Martin (2018) asked in her grounded theory study on the perceptions of employees, as stakeholders, of the businesses regarding the impact of working for BAMs, "Why is there so little written about the impact on the employees' lives, female or male, in the presently available literature, particularly, the female employees?" (p. 53) C. M. Martin performed her research with a feminist lens from a unique perspective of Indonesian female employees working for international female Christian entrepreneurs. On Java Island, Indonesia, 33 female Indonesian employees working for four BAM firms owned or managed by international female Christian entrepreneurs participated in the study. Many of the participants were former factory workers, domestic helpers, and farm laborers. The four BAM businesses consisted of a textile business, an English language preschool, and early primary school, a bead and jewelry production firm, and an additional textile business (C. M. Martin, 2018).

Each of these four enterprises was founded when foreign or expatriate women saw a need. C. M. Martin (2018) referred to them as "spontaneous BAM enterprises" (p. 87).

As the central conclusion of her study, C. M. Martin (2018) discovered that the participants, as stakeholders of the four BAM businesses, perceived their work to be "comfortable, at ease, safe, and secure" (p. 114) in terms of providing financial support for their families, acquiring new job skills, and fostering relationships. However, the participants perceived barriers to conversion to Christianity due to the fact that their spouses adhered to the Islamic faith and were the "head of the family" (C. M. Martin, 2018, p. 154). C. M. Martin (2018) found that if men and wives were not ministered together, it would be difficult for the BAMs to attain their spiritual bottom line. Consequently, "relationship building with Muslims" (p. 155) became critical. Participants in an Islamic context also perceived tensions between the Christian faith and their traditional culture (p. 155–156). Therefore, it was crucial to build bridges between Muslim culture and the gospel (p. 157).

On the other hand, the participants in C. M. Martin's (2018) study, as stakeholders of the BAMs, perceived the weekly Bible classes as a means of relationship building that was "of great significance" to the participants' BAM experiences, but the researcher discovered that "BAM literature has paid little attention to" this phenomenon (p. 272). One attendee stated, "The weekly Bible teaching times and fellowship strengthens our relationships" (p. 167). The employees perceived their employers, the international female

Christian entrepreneurs, as servants and dependable companions (p. 169–171). The participants also perceived working for international female Christian entrepreneurs to provide a healthier work-life balance than their previous employment (C. M. Martin, 2018). The participants were thrilled with the work experiences and skills they acquired while working with BAMs, as well as their ability to work from home while caring for their children (C. M. Martin, 2018, pp. 206–207). Lastly, the participants perceived earning a living as "empowerment and autonomy" (C. M. Martin, 2018, p. 265).

In another empirical study conducted in Odisha, India, Devarapalli (2020) applied the Pauline model of business as ministry in an indigenous context and introduced a new term called "native tentmaking" (p.3). The study explored tentmaking, a form of business as ministry, with twenty-six undergraduate students and ten Christian workers educated locally by the Training in Evangelism Needs and Technology organization (Devarapalli, 2020). Participants in the study established for-profit micro-businesses as native tentmakers with initial financing from family and community members. They perceived the businesses as a Christian ministry calling "just like any calling to vocation or ministry" (Devarapalli, 2020, p. 95). However, the majority of participants lacked business development expertise and abilities and found it difficult to maintain a balance between ministry and business. Six participants endured persecution in the form of physical assaults as well as the destruction of their property and animals at the hands of local religious fundamentalists intent on severing the revenue sources of Christian workers. Due to the persecution, a number of microbusinesses lost operating capital (Devarapalli, 2020, p. 82). Twenty-one stakeholders of the microbusinesses perceived the businesses as ministry as "spiritual challenges" with the experiences of "depression, anxiety, and confusion about their callings to microbusiness as well as disturbances in their relationships" (Devarapalli, 2020, p. 104).

Rundle and Lee (2022) recently conducted a survey study with 119 participants to identify the "characteristics, best practices, or impact of business as mission (BAM) practitioners and businesses" using a "grounded typology of four distinct types of BAM practitioners" for the purpose of understanding the personal and contextual factors that contribute to the impact and sustainability of a BAM enterprise (p. 436). Despite the fact that the 119 participants were limited to "self-defined BAM practitioners" (p. 421), predominantly from England and the United States (p. 437), the study created a theoretical framework for a more comprehensive and nuanced understanding of BAM. In this framework, missional identity salience (affiliation with mission agency) and business identity salience (rationalized business practices) were utilized to form a matrix in two dimensions. With "Low" and "High" assigned to each dimension, four types of BAM practitioners were categorized as "BAMers" (for-profit business owners with a personification of BAM—"High" in missional and "High" in business), "Evangelists" (missionaries with a missional identity—"High" in missional and "Low" in business), Faith-Driven Entrepreneurs (FDEs) (the tentmakers with more work or business experience—"Low" in missional and "High" in business), and Explorers (newcomers— "Low" in missional and "Low" in business) (p. 425–429). In the study, the most noteworthy finding is that BAM practitioners with varied social identities have proportionally different perceptions of how each of the four "bottom lines" of economic, social, spiritual, and environmental effects should be prioritized. FDEs prefer economic outcomes, Evangelists prefer spiritual outcomes, BAMers are balanced between the two, while Explorers are still unbalanced in either area. Based on their social identity, work experience, and management techniques, the typological paradigm anticipates fundamental disparities in how BAM practitioners "do mission" and "do business" (Rundle & Lee, 2022, p. 436).

Sorenson and Milbrandt (2023) conducted an empirical study to investigate the association between family faith, family values, and business family social capital within the context of family-owned enterprises. The research conducted by the authors is grounded in comprehensive qualitative research involving four distinct owning families who are allied with various Christian denominations. According to the authors, family social capital is conceptualized as the reservoir of resources inherent in familial relationships, which can be harnessed to accomplish personal, familial, and entrepreneurial objectives. The authors contended that the presence of familial faith beliefs can have a significant impact on enhancing family values and, in turn, business family social capital.

The findings of the authors indicated that family faith has a positive impact on family values through three distinct mechanisms. First, the presence of shared beliefs: The faith tradition within a family serves as a unifying force, fostering a collective adherence to a set of beliefs and values that can bring family members together and inform their decision-making processes. Second, shared practices encompass many family faith practices, including but not limited to attending traditional faith services, engaging in communal prayers, and collectively studying scripture. These practices serve to fortify family values and foster the development of robust interpersonal bonds. Third, shared narratives: The utilization of family faith tales and traditions can facilitate the transmission of family values to subsequent generations.

The researchers additionally discovered that family values contribute to the enhancement of social capital within business families through three distinct mechanisms. First, trust: The cultivation of family values, such as honesty, integrity, and fairness, can contribute to the establishment of trust within familial relationships, as well as among employees and other relevant stakeholders. Second, communication: The promotion of family values can foster an environment of transparent and sincere communication within the familial enterprise. Third, commitment: The cultivation of family values can cultivate a sense of commitment and responsibility throughout family members and employees.

The authors suggested that business family social capital has the potential to yield various favorable consequences, such as: First, the succession of family businesses: The utilization of social capital within business families can facilitate a seamless transfer of leadership from one generation to the subsequent. Second, the impact of business family social capital on business performance: The presence of business family social capital has been found to have a positive influence on business performance through its facilitation of innovation, creativity, and cooperation. Third, community support: Family enterprises characterized by substantial levels of business family social capital exhibit a greater propensity to engage in and provide assistance to their immediate communities.

The study conducted by Sorenson and Milbrandt (2023) yielded results that indicated the potential for family faith to have a beneficial impact on family enterprises. Specifically, it was seen that family faith can contribute to the reinforcement of family values, consequently enhancing the social capital within the business family. Familyowned businesses that prioritize and uphold family values while fostering an environment characterized by trust, congruent communication, and unwavering dedication are more inclined to achieve sustainability in the long run (Sorenson & Milbrandt, 2023).

Summary of Business as Ministry

Illuminated from the narrative of the Book of Acts in the Bible, the business owned by Priscilla and Aquila might be a solely-for-profit business before they were converted to Christianity. The Apostle Paul, as a tentmaking professional, supported himself financially for his missions by working as a business partner with Priscilla and Aquila. After Priscilla and Aquila were converted to Christianity, the business of the three tentmakers might be transformed into a marketplace ministry, a form of business as ministry, under the CG model with a quadruple bottom-line approach. One of their ministries was discipleship for Apollos. When Priscilla and Aquila relocated their business from Corinth to Ephesus and Apollos was sent to Achaia as a missionary, their business as ministry was developed into a form of business as mission. These Pauline models of business as ministry in the early church were the prototypes of various forms of business as ministry in modern churches. The core of business as ministry is the common good of business, and the common good itself is a Kingdom business (McVea & Naughton, 2021; Sison & Fontrodona, 2011). The performance of a Kingdom business can be measured by the common good matrix and the common good balance sheet (Felber et al., 2019). The concept of wisdom business is glorifying God and developing people (Stolze, 2021) as well as restoration and reconciliation of relationships of God-human, human-human, and human-nature.

Summary of Literature Review

This chapter provides a historical, cultural, and religious context for the rural Midwest of the United States, as well as a literature review of several theoretical frameworks and empirical research for understanding the phenomenon of business as ministry for the common good. In this study, the classification of business models of profitmaking organizations assisted in identifying the characteristics of a business and evaluating their contributions to the common good. The scope and forms of business as ministry and relevant empirical studies were reviewed.

Nonetheless, the literature review found that the prevailing body of literature pertaining to the integration of business and Christian ministry for the common good predominantly represented the viewpoints of individuals engaged in international missions or those involved in urban settings regarding the underlying purposes of business. Limited knowledge existed regarding the practices and perceptions of business as ministry stakeholders in the rural Midwestern United States concerning the concept of the common good.

Chapter 3

Methodology

This chapter presents a comprehensive examination of the research processes and methodologies employed in this basic qualitative study aimed at understanding how the business as ministry stakeholders in the rural Midwestern United States practice and perceive the common good. In this discussion, I will expound upon the qualitative research approach employed, the methods of data collection and selection of participants, the process of data analysis, considerations of trustworthiness, ethical concerns, and the researcher's positionality.

Research Paradigm and Approach

According to Glesne (2016), research paradigms can be seen as a theoretical framework or philosophical perspective within the field of science. These paradigms are characterized by their underlying assumptions about the nature of reality and truth, the types of inquiries to be pursued, and the methodologies employed in the research process. In essence, a research paradigm embodies the philosophical assumptions held by a researcher in relation to fundamental inquiries, such as the nature of reality. How can knowledge be acquired? What is the methodology employed for determining the answer?

In what manner do one's views influence their conduct as a researcher?

Research Paradigm

Creswell and Poth (2017) asserted that qualitative research paradigms comprise several theoretical frameworks, namely postpositivism, social constructivism, the transformative framework, and postmodern perspectives.

Social constructivism is commonly perceived as an interpretive framework. Social constructivism is a theoretical framework wherein individuals endeavor to gain an understanding of the world in which they reside and engage in professional activities. Individuals construct subjective interpretations of their experiences, specifically interpretations that are relevant to particular objects or entities. The interpretations include a wide range of perspectives, necessitating the researcher to thoroughly analyze the multitude of viewpoints instead of simplifying them into a limited number of categories or concepts. Therefore, the primary aim of this study is to place significant emphasis on the perspectives of the participants in order to address the research topic. The subjective definitions in question are often subject to recurrent disputes from both social and historical standpoints. In essence, these constructs are not solely ingrained in individuals but rather emerge through interpersonal engagement (thus, social construction) and are shaped by the historical and cultural standards that operate inside individuals' experiences. Instead of commencing with a theoretical framework, such as postpositivism, researchers build or develop a theory or pattern of meaning using inductive reasoning (Creswell & Poth, 2017).

Based on the nature of the research question, the context of this study, and my personal experiences, the present study adopted a social constructivist perspective. This theoretical framework posits that there is no singular, objective, or observable reality or truth external to individuals. The interpretations of reality are subjective, relative, complex, diverse, and ontologically produced within a social context (Costantino, 2008; Creswell & Creswell, 2018; Glesne, 2016; Merriam & Tisdell, 2016). The epistemological stance of social constructivism posits that knowledge is produced by human interactions within specific historical and socio-cultural contexts (Costantino, 2008; Merriam & Tisdell, 2016).

In accordance with this theoretical framework, my research stance towards this dissertation was characterized by a receptiveness to the diverse range of perspectives and issues that may emerge (Glesne, 2016). The primary objective of qualitative research is to gain a comprehensive understanding of the subjective and diverse interpretations of participants' experiences instead of testing an established theory (Merriam & Tisdell, 2016).

This basic qualitative study aimed to understand how the business as ministry stakeholders in the rural Midwestern United States practiced and perceived business as ministry for the common good. This study refrained from making assumptions regarding the stakeholders' exposure to a singular perception of business as ministry for the common good. This study aimed to explore the diverse perspectives and understandings of stakeholders in relation to their experiences of business as ministry in the rural areas of the

US Midwest. Hence, I utilized a social constructivism paradigm as the theoretical framework for my qualitative research design in this study.

Research Approach

The selection of methodology and research approach is contingent upon the inherent characteristics of the research question. The primary research question of this study pertains to the stakeholders of business as ministry in the US Midwestern rural region and their perceptions of the concept of the common good. According to Merriam and Tisdell (2016), employing a basic qualitative research approach is highly appropriate for the objective of this study, which aimed to gain insight into individuals' interpretations of their lives and experiences. In comparison to alternative qualitative research methodologies, the basic qualitative research method served as a valuable research tool for acquiring a full comprehension of the experiences and interpretations of those engaged in business as ministry within the specific setting of the US Midwest.

In the qualitative paradigm, the generation of knowledge is a collaborative effort between the researcher and the participants, occurring throughout the research process. The researcher assumes a pivotal role as a major instrument in facilitating this process (Costantino, 2008; Creswell & Creswell, 2018; Creswell & Poth, 2017; Glesne, 2016; Merriam & Tisdell, 2016). The role of a qualitative researcher is crucial in the collection and analysis of data during the entirety of the study. According to Merriam and Tisdell (2016), the researcher has the ability to provide prompt feedback, modify their approach, analyze both verbal and non-verbal cues, and seek clarification from the individuals involved in the research. This methodology enables the researcher to establish a close collaboration with the participants in order to gain a comprehensive understanding of their experiences. The aforementioned attributes of a basic qualitative research methodology exhibited a strong alignment with the parameters of the present study.

According to Creswell and Poth (2017), qualitative research is characterized by the initial establishment of assumptions and the utilization of interpretive or theoretical frameworks. These frameworks serve as a foundation for investigating research questions that try to understand the subjective meaning attributed by individuals or groups to social or human issues. The typical context for qualitative research is usually the setting where participants experience the issue, with the primary instrument being the researcher themselves (Creswell & Poth, 2017). The research methodology employed in this study was qualitative in nature, utilizing an inductive approach. This strategy involved building upon abstract units, such as categories or themes, that are derived from the data. The fieldwork was carried out in the state of Iowa, which is situated in the United States Midwest region, where the participants experienced business as ministry. Hence, employing a basic qualitative research methodology is deemed most suitable for this particular study.

Data Collection and Analysis

This study utilized many methods, including observation, interviews, and data mining from papers and artifacts, to gather information. In the subsequent sections, a comprehensive data collection strategies and methodologies will be presented.

Participant Selection

This research has gathered data from a sample size ranging of 33 stakeholders representing 14 enterprises practicing business as ministry. The participants were selected from a pool of small businesses and farms located in Iowa, United States. These enterprises and farms were actively involved in conducting business as ministry. In pursuit of business as ministry for the common good, they amalgamated profit-making enterprises with Christian ministry. My objective was to foster a sense of connection and mutual understanding with the participants by actively engaging in volunteer farm work. Through the network in local faith-based organizations and social media, I utilized a snowball sampling technique to solicit introductions to other stakeholders associated with the businesses under studied. I constructed an elaborate exposition of my research, elucidating the rationale for its necessity and the potential advantages that local enterprises and ministry practitioners may accrue from its investigation. I obtained approval from the Institutional Review Board (IRB) before data collection.

The present study employed intentional sampling as a methodological approach to identify information-rich examples. This facilitated the provision of a comprehensive and complete account of the central phenomenon under study and addressed the research questions at hand (Merriam & Tisdell, 2016). In order to initiate intentional sampling, I established the specific criteria for the selection of the samples. These criteria were closely aligned with the objectives of the study and served as a guiding framework for identifying cases that provide a rich and relevant information field (Merriam & Tisdell, 2016). In order to be eligible for inclusion in this study, participants were required to satisfy the following criteria: First, in order to participate in an independent interview, individuals must be at least 18 years of age. Second, business or farm owners that engage in profit-making business operations while incorporating Christian ministry principles. Third, other stakeholders of business as ministry, namely employees, customers, suppliers, contractors, competitors, ministry partners, service recipients, and members of the local community.

Fourth, they were residing or being employed in the rural Midwest region of the United

States, with a particular preference for the state of Iowa.

Data Collection

Within the scope of this research endeavor. The primary methods employed for data collection in this study were participant observation and semi-structured interviews. According to Merriam and Tisdell (2016), qualitative research relies on observations as a fundamental source of data. This is because observational data provides a direct and unmediated experience with the naturally occurring event of interest. Engaging in various farm works such as planting, fertilizing, harvesting, and maintaining farm equipment, as well as participating in events promoting water and soil conservation, and Christian ministries including worship services, Bible study groups, and sharing Bible verses after horseback riding lessons, provided me with the opportunity to observe how my research participants actively implemented the concept of the common good through practicing business as ministry. Additionally, the distribution of farm produce to churches, food pantries, and customers allowed me to witness firsthand the practical application of this approach within the context of a naturally occurring phenomenon of interest. During the course of the observation fieldwork, I diligently maintained a journal and promptly recorded field notes either contemporaneously with the observation or at the earliest opportunity. I utilized my mobile device, employing the voice dictation functionality, to document field observations and transcribe the recorded interviews. Additionally, I have developed a series of observational techniques for the purpose of data collecting. The interview transcripts were processed using Dedoose, a qualitative data analysis software developed by the University of California, Los Angeles, specifically designed for the purpose of qualitative and mixed data analysis.

In addition to making observations, interviews served as a crucial means of gathering data to gain a comprehensive understanding of the subject being investigated in this qualitative study (Merriam & Tisdell, 2016). In the past few years, the utilization of video-conferencing software for online interviews has presented novel issues pertaining to reflexivity (Flick, 2022).

These challenges will be further examined in the subsequent section on Trustworthiness. The interview tactics encompassed several formats, such as one-on-one, in-person, and online interviews. The interviews followed a semi-structured format, utilizing an interview protocol that included obtaining oral agreement from participants and ensuring the use of pseudonyms for anonymity. One iteration of the interview guide was designed specifically for business owners, focusing on gathering data regarding their experiences and perceptions in their roles as both founders and employers (see to Appendix A). A supplementary iteration of the interview guide was developed to cater to stakeholders outside the business owners, including employees, customers, suppliers, service recipients, and members of the community. This version primarily gathered data based on participants' personal experiences and perceptions related to the business as ministry they involved. For further details, please refer to Appendix B. The predominant method employed for notetaking during the interviews was audio recording.

Data Storage and Confidentiality

Effective data storage is a critical aspect of research due to the substantial volume of data that necessitates preservation and analysis inside personal or institutional cloudbased platforms. In accordance with the recommendations put forward by Creswell and Poth (2017) regarding data storage and management, I ensured the creation of two backup copies of the data by utilizing both personal cloud and university cloud storage solutions.

Two audio recorders were utilized, each equipped with ample data storage capacity for audio recording. Subsequently, the recorded files were transferred to Dedoose, a software platform, following each data gathering session. I compiled a comprehensive inventory of the gathered data. The audio files, field notes, and interview transcripts were saved within the Dedoose platform. In order to uphold the privacy and confidentiality of my participants, pseudonyms were employed for all data storage. This measure was implemented to ensure data security and adhere to the requirements set forth by the Institutional Review Board

(IRB).

Data Analysis

According to Flick (2014), the process of data analysis involves categorizing and interpreting linguistic or visual content in order to draw conclusions about the underlying dimensions and patterns of meaning within the material, as well as the representations conveyed by it. The importance of doing data collecting and analysis concurrently in qualitative research has been emphasized by Merriam and Tisdell (2016). This approach has proven to be time-efficient in the processing of data in this study. The problem statement was taken into consideration during the selection of a purposeful sample in order to collect data that would effectively address the issue both within and outside of the field. As a result in this study, the analysis of data during the data collection process yielded findings that were both concise and enlightening. The objective of the data analysis was to ascertain responses to the research inquiries. The aforementioned responses were alternatively referred to as categories, themes, or findings in the subsequent chapters.

In this study, the researcher primarily adhered to the procedure recommended by Creswell and Poth (2017), which they referred to as "a data analysis spiral" (p.248). This approach involves several steps, including: First, data collection—which entails transcribing raw data obtained from observations, interviews, and documents, engaging in reading and note-taking, employing visual aids and textual analysis, summarizing field notes, and engaging in reflective thinking. Second, managing and organizing the data—this involves digitizing the information and categorizing it into searchable files, labeling these files based on a spreadsheet that contains participant information, data forms, and collection details, among other relevant data. Third, gaining a comprehensive understanding of the entire database by engaging in a process of reading and note-taking, utilizing memos to capture emerging concepts. Fourth, establishing codes or categories by providing descriptions and categorizations of codes and organizing them into overarching themes. Finally, interpreting the data and critically evaluating the interpretations in order to ascertain the insights and knowledge gained from the analysis. The data is transformed into textual, tabular, or graphical formats to represent and visualize the information effectively. In this stage, the researcher had the opportunity to gather feedback on the initial summaries and data displays from informants by redistributing the material to them (Creswell & Poth, 2017, pp. 254–266).

For transcribing audio records, I used technological aids such as Google Pixel 4 cellphone, Microsoft's Dictate, or Otter.ai in addition to the traditional manual transcribing for field notes and interviews.

Coding—The concept of coding in qualitative research, as defined by Saldaña (2021), refers to the practice of assigning a word or brief phrase that represents a concise, significant, essence-capturing, and evocative characteristic to a specific segment of language-based or visual data. According to Merriam and Tisdell (2016), the purpose of organizing data in a specific manner is to facilitate the retrieval of specific bits of information. This study employed a basic qualitative approach, wherein the coding procedure outlined by Merriam and Tisdell (2016) was predominantly utilized. Specifically, their "step-by-step process of analysis" (p.204) served as the guiding framework for this research. In a basic descriptive study, the analytical procedure known as the "step-by-step process of analysis" encompasses three primary stages: initial coding, sometimes referred to as open coding, focused coding, and thematic coding. According to Merriam and Tisdell (2016), coding can be characterized as a dialectical process involving the interplay between a macro-level perspective, which encompasses the overall context or the "forest" and a micro-level focus on specific details or the "trees" (Merriam & Tisdell, 2016, p. 207).

Initial coding—The initial coding phase involved the examination of the initial interview transcripts, the first set of field notes, and the first document gathered during the research. During the preliminary coding phase, the data segments consisted of languagebased or visual elements, such as

observation field notes, interviews, and archival documents. The first coding

procedure commenced with a conceptualization of "trees" as a metaphorical

framework. The data set was thereafter examined on an incident-by-incident

basis, with particular attention given to identifying the predominant themes

pertaining to the interaction or dialogue within the data set. Through the

process of analyzing individual "trees," I gathered data that encompassed a

pertinent term or phrase serving as a code that aligned with my research

inquiries. During the initial coding phase, the researcher replicated the same

words or phrases spoken by the subject. On few occasions, I utilized a

specific term or notion that accurately conveys their subjective perceptions.

This method is commonly referred to as in vivo coding, which allows

researchers to accurately capture and retain the participants' interpretations of

their sensations during the coding process

(Charmaz, 2014).

Focused coding—Focused coding entails selecting the most relevant

codes from the initial coding step and categorizing them. This procedure aids

in the refinement of the analysis and the identification of the most important

themes in the data. The primary objective of my analysis was to identify the

most prominent codes exhibiting a recurring pattern within the dataset. I

proceeded to assess the first codes that showed the highest level of analytical

coherence, enabling me to successfully organize the data into distinct categories. These categories were subsequently assigned a new coding word for better categorization (Merriam & Tisdell, 2016, p. 207).

Thematic coding—Thematic coding is the process of discovering the overarching themes that arise from the focused coding stage. This procedure aids in developing a deeper knowledge of the facts and drawing conclusions regarding the issue under investigation. This aim prompted me to consider the following inquiry: What are the primary themes that manifest when contemplating my study? What are the primary insights that I have acquired? What are the responses to the research inquiries posed by the study participants? The formation of a forest can be seen as an example of how trees come together to represent a broader ecological system in nature. Similarly, the synthesis of themes through the use of codes can provide light on a wider set of data (Charmaz, 2014).

Constant comparative analysis—Recommended by Merriam and Tisdell (2016), the process of constant comparative analysis was employed, wherein I revisited the individual data bits, represented by the "trees," subsequent to the deforestation of the "forest." The purpose was to ascertain whether these data bits align with the overall patterns and observations derived from the "forest," thereby facilitating a comprehensive and ongoing comparative study. Through a persistent analysis of the similarities and differences between individual "trees" and the collective entity of a "forest," the themes derived from this study were condensed into a smaller number of all-encompassing categories as the findings of this study. The researcher also employed constant comparative analysis to establish connections between the findings and the existing literature, so generating novel insights that contribute to the existing body of knowledge in the relevant academic disciplines.

Trustworthiness

Guba and Lincoln (1994) claimed that there are some associations between positivist paradigms of inquiry and naturalistic inquiry. In this regard, quantitative approaches are oriented toward the attainment of internal validity, whereas qualitative methods prioritize the establishment of credibility. Qualitative methodologies strive to achieve transferability, while quantitative methodologies aim to attain generalizability. In contrast to quantitative methodologies that prioritize reliability, qualitative research methods aim to achieve dependability. Qualitative methodologies aim to establish confirmability, whereas quantitative methodologies prioritize objectivity. The researcher's objective in addressing these concerns was to demonstrate the trustworthiness of the findings and convince readers of their accuracy, as noted by Creswell and Poth (2017). According to Guba and Lincoln (1994), trustworthiness can be classified into four main dimensions: credibility, transferability, dependability, and confirmability.

Credibility

The concept of credibility, as defined by Schwandt (2015), pertains to the alignment between the participants' perspectives on their life events and the reconstruction and portrayal of these experiences by the researcher.

Academic researchers employ various methodologies to establish their credibility. These methodologies include thorough engagement in data collection, consistent observation, triangulation, peer debriefing, examination of discrepant data, referential adequacy, member checking, maintenance of a reflexive journal, and meticulous analysis of researchers' own perspectives. In accordance with the suggestion put forth by Merriam and Tisdell (2016), I employed several rationales in my particular context to establish credibility. These included thorough engagement in data collection and analysis, consistent observation, triangulation, examination of discrepant data, member checking, maintenance of a reflexive journal, and meticulous analysis of researchers' own perspectives.

Thorough Engagement in Data

According to Merriam and Tisdell (2016), thorough engagement in data collection and analysis can justify establishing credibility based on a broad timeline. With more than two years of living experience in the Midwestern United States, the researcher actively engaged in agricultural work over an entire growing season. Additionally, the researcher regularly observed the participants' YouTube channel, averaging three times per week over the course of a year, in order to gain insights into their lived experiences across all four seasons. The transcripts of the interviews conducted with all 33 participants in this study were meticulously compiled by the researcher in order to establish a compelling argument for sustained involvement with the collected data (Merriam & Tisdell, 2016).

Triangulation

Triangulation is a method employed to enhance the credibility of the data utilized in the process of drawing conclusions. To comprehensively examine a result from several perspectives, it may be imperative to employ multiple sources of data, researchers, theoretical frameworks, or procedures for data analysis (Schwandt, 2015). This study involved the analysis of primary data obtained from field research encompassing interview transcripts, field notes, and archived documents, complemented by the use of secondary data from existing literature. The purpose of incorporating secondary data was to triangulate and enhance the comprehension of the original data. For example, the comprehensive analysis of the 1980s Midwest farm crisis was conducted by examining the perspectives of multiple farmers who directly encountered this phenomenon. This approach aimed to gain a thorough understanding of the available data. A total of fourteen research sites were employed in order to achieve triangulation. Family history, books, historical newspapers, newsletters, and graduate theses were collected and analyzed during the process of triangulation.

Researcher Reflexivity

Researcher reflexivity encompasses the practice of acknowledging and critically examining the biases and preconceptions held by the researcher. This approach has the potential to mitigate the influence of bias on both the research process and the resulting findings. (Creswell & Poth, 2017). Throughout the entirety of the study process, I diligently maintained a reflexive journal. The utilization of reflexivity in the research process facilitated the enhancement of the researcher's awareness regarding personal biases and assumptions. This practice also fostered transparency and accountability during the inductive research process. Furthermore, reflexivity contributed to the development of a more profound comprehension of the collected data. Additionally, it engendered novel insights and perspectives pertaining to the research topic. Lastly, reflexivity constituted an integral component of the meticulous analysis of the researchers' own perspectives.

Transferability

Transferability, as defined by Merriam and Tisdell (2016), pertains to the extent to which the results of a study can be extrapolated and applied to different contexts or settings. The concept of transferability holds significant importance in qualitative research as it enables researchers to assert the extent to which their findings may be applied to different contexts. Nevertheless, it is crucial to acknowledge that transferability should not be conflated with quantitative generalizability. In the context of quantitative research, the concept of generalizability pertains to the capacity to extend the conclusions derived from a specific sample to a broader population. Transferability in qualitative research relates to the capacity to extend the findings of a study to alternative contexts or settings.

In this research endeavor, significant endeavors were undertaken to augment the transferability of the outcomes. These efforts encompassed the careful selection of a representative sample, the meticulous collection of comprehensive and complete data and contextual information, the thorough documentation of the research method, and a conscientious examination of the researcher's personal biases and assumptions.

Thick Description

Thick description refers to a comprehensive and meticulous account of the research setting, individuals involved, and the methodologies employed. The inclusion of detailed and comprehensive descriptions is crucial in order to enable readers to assess the extent to which the findings of a study can be applied to their own specific circumstances (Creswell & Poth, 2017). In the present chapter, a comprehensive account of the study methodologies employed is provided, including participant recruitment, data collection, and data analysis. Chapter 4 comprises an elaborate exposition of the research context, encompassing the delineation of the site, participants, and cultural aspects. In the chapters of data analysis, findings, and implications, I employed in vivo coding to provide a rich and thick description of this work.

Data Saturation

Data saturation refers to the stage in qualitative research where the collection of data from participants reaches a point of saturation, indicating that no new information or insights are being obtained. Ensuring data saturation is a crucial step in the research process as it allows for the development of conclusions that are grounded in a full comprehension of the topic under research (Creswell & Poth, 2017). In the present study, data saturation was achieved, encompassing a total of 33 participants from 14 business entities, extended from planned 20 participants and 5 business entities. Consequently, the cessation of data collection from participants was indicated. Data saturation was evaluated by the identification of recurring patterns and themes within the dataset, as well as by soliciting additional input from participants regarding any additional information they wished to contribute.

Theoretical Grounding

The incorporation of theoretical grounding in research enhances the transferability of the findings. Theory serves as a conceptual structure that facilitates comprehension and analysis of evidence, while also enabling the formulation of testable theoretical framework in diverse settings (Creswell & Poth, 2017). In the present study, a comprehensive examination was conducted, wherein pertinent literature was thoroughly evaluated and constantly compared to ascertain suitable theoretical frameworks that might be employed to inform the research. The use of theoretical frameworks had a pivotal role in formulating my research inquiries, interpreting the outcomes of my study, and constructing my own theoretical framework in the common good treasure conceptualization.

Dependability

Schwandt (2015) asserts that the concept of dependability incorporates the methodical nature of the research process and the imperative for the researcher to ensure logical coherence, traceability, and comprehensive documentation. The concept of dependability holds significant importance in qualitative research as it enables researchers to assert the trustworthiness of their findings. Additionally, this practice enables other researchers to reproduce the study and verify the obtained results.

In this study, the researcher exerted significant effort to enhance the dependability of the research findings through the implementation of a rigorous research design and methodology. Additionally, the researcher demonstrated transparency in regards to the research process, as advocated by Shenton (2004). To further strengthen the dependability of the study, data from multiple sources were triangulated. Furthermore, the study underwent a review process by two researchers affiliated with local universities in the Midwestern United States, as suggested by Terrell (2016).

Prolonged Engagement

Creswell and Poth (2017) propose that prolonged engagement implicates a substantial investment of time in the research setting, fostering extensive interaction with participants, and diligently gathering data. This facilitates the researcher in cultivating a profound comprehension of the topic under study and mitigating the potential for erroneous interpretation of the findings. During the course of this study, a substantial portion of time was dedicated to conducting fieldwork, engaging with study participants, and gathering empirical data. This facilitated the cultivation of a profound comprehension of the topic under study and mitigated the potential for data misinterpretation.

Consistent Observation

The process of consistent observation involves the identification of recurring patterns and themes that arise from the data. There are several methodologies available to do this task, including coding, thematic analysis, and content analysis (Saldaña, 2021). The maintenance of consistent observation holds significant importance in qualitative research as it serves to uphold the dependability and credibility of the obtained findings. Additionally, Flick (2014) suggests that it is beneficial to discern the most significant and meaningful elements of the data. In this study, the duration of field observations was extended, and the sample size was increased in order to facilitate the consistent emergence of recurrent patterns and themes.

Examination of Discrepant Data

The examination of discrepant data involves the identification and exploration of data that deviates from the initial research findings. This may encompass data that presents contradictions to the established conclusions, as well as evidence that is unexpected or without explanation (Flick, 2014). The analysis of inconsistent data holds significance within the qualitative research methodology, as it contributes to the dependability and credibility of research outcomes, ensuring their comprehensiveness and accuracy. Additionally, it might be beneficial in the identification of novel insights and unexplored domains for further research (Merriam & Tisdell, 2016). In this study, a comparison was conducted between discrepant data and data obtained from other participants pertaining to the same topics. Additionally, a comparative analysis was conducted between the data obtained in this study and those derived from other relevant studies. Moreover, an examination was performed on the contextual factors surrounding the acquisition of the incongruous data, including the demographic characteristics of the participants, the specific study environment, and the methodology employed during the interviews. The presence of discrepant data has provided me with novel insights and has opened up new avenues for future research.

Confirmability

Schwandt (2015) defines confirmability as the aim of guaranteeing that the data and interpretations obtained from an investigation are not influenced by the subjective constructs of the researcher's imagination. Confirmability is a crucial and fundamental notion within the realm of qualitative research, as it enables researchers to assert objectivity and lack of bias in their findings. Additionally, it facilitates the opportunity for other researchers to scrutinize the research methodology and corroborate the results.

In this study, the researcher exerted significant effort to augment the confirmability of the findings through meticulous documentation of the research method, utilization of numerous data sources and triangulation, and presentation of ample evidence to substantiate the findings.

Member Checking

Guba and Lincoln (1994) asserted that member checking is the most important form of confirmability and credibility as it gives importance to the subject's voice. In order to satisfy the need for confirmability, member checking refers to asking respondents for feedback on a researcher's results (Schwandt, 2015). In this study, member checking was the process of making sure I fully comprehend my subjects or that I was accurately interpreting their voices. I conducted the member checking while collecting the data by providing the transcripts and audio recordings of their interviews. For those participants for whom I was not able to conduct member checking during data collection, I provided opportunities for member checking during data analysis to get a deeper insight into how they perceive my interpretation (Merriam & Tisdell, 2016) by offering study participants an opportunity to review my complete dissertation. I have received some feedback.

Audit Trail

According to Creswell and Poth (2017), an audit trail refers to a comprehensive documentation of the research process, including the researcher's choices, activities, and analyses. The comprehensive compilation should cover all pertinent information, comprising field notes, transcripts, and analytical notes. Researchers enable others to replicate and evaluate the dependability of their findings by furnishing an audit trail. Throughout this study, I consistently and conscientiously maintained a research journal to record my decision-making process, actions, and interpretations. The utilization of this journal might facilitate the establishment of an audit trail, enabling subsequent researchers to comprehend and trace the progression of my work.

Peer Review

Creswell and Poth (2017) assert that peer review comprehends the systematic evaluation and constructive critique of a study's outcomes by fellow researchers. The process of peer review plays a crucial role in the identification of potential biases and inaccuracies within the research process, thereby enhancing the confirmability of the findings. In this study, a doctoral candidate who was familiar with the research methods and two university professors who were also local Midwestern farmers and thus "familiar with the phenomenon explored" (Creswell & Poth, 2017, p. 325) conducted reviews of my complete dissertation. The reviewers offered constructive criticism regarding the research procedures and findings, perhaps enhancing the confirmability of this work.

After careful consideration of developing a qualitative research design that incorporates the four fundamental criteria of credibility, transferability, dependability, and confirmability, it became evident that the strategies that fulfill these criteria frequently overlapped with the broader components of the research design. To ensure my research's credibility, transferability, dependability, and confirmability, I have incorporated various methodological strategies. These included engaging extensively with the data, employing triangulation techniques, practicing researcher reflexivity, providing detailed and comprehensive descriptions, achieving data saturation, grounding the study in relevant theoretical frameworks, maintaining prolonged engagement with the research participants, consistently observing the phenomena under investigation, examining any discrepant data, seeking member validation, documenting an audit trail, and subjecting the research to peer review.

Ethical Issues

Ethical dilemmas occur in qualitative research when researchers recognize that their comprehensive efforts may potentially have negative consequences on the well-being and lived experiences of the individuals involved in the study (Miles et al., 2019). The research participants made a significant contribution to the present study by willingly and voluntarily participating in the research. Hence, it was reasonable to demonstrate appreciation and esteem towards the study participants for their valuable contributions of time, experiences, insights, and privacy. To demonstrate appreciation for the significant contributions made by the participants of my research, who generously shared their lived experiences and insights, I remained dedicated to upholding a strong level of expertise, conscientiousness, and meticulousness in my capacity as a researcher throughout the duration of my study.

The principle of "do no harm," as articulated by Merriam and Tisdell (2016, p.

261), was consistently upheld in my thoughts and actions. Ensuring the safety and safeguarding of the right to privacy of study participants held significant importance in my perspective. Before doing any formal study, I obtained the necessary approval for my dissertation proposal from the Institutional Review Board (IRB). In adherence to the guidelines set forth by the IRB, I utilized the Biola University Consent to Act as A Human study Participant's

Informed Consent Form template, which was duly authorized by the IRB. For

further reference, please consult Appendix C and D. Prior to doing any

formal research with individual participants, written informed consent was

obtained from the participant by the signature of the Informed Consent Form.

The concept of informed consent entails that individuals who partake in

research must acquire comprehensive information regarding the research

procedures, as well as the potential advantages and disadvantages associated

with their participation, prior to providing their assent. In this study, the

researcher ensured the preservation of the participants' confidentiality by

refraining from disclosing participants' names or any other identifying details

without their explicit consent. Additionally, the researcher took measures to

eliminate participants' names and other identifying information from

transcripts and employed pseudonyms in all written materials pertaining to

this study. All study participants were provided with prior notification that

their involvement is completely voluntary, and they retain the freedom to

terminate their participation at any given point. The researcher provided

explicit assurances to the study participants regarding the methods and

locations employed to safeguard and protect all collected data, so ensuring

that exclusive access to the original data is maintained solely by the

researcher. Furthermore, the researcher took measures to ensure that the

study participants' viewpoints, opinions, and personal narratives were solely utilized for research objectives. The researcher effectively conveyed in a manner that engender confidence among the study participants.

Positionality

A researcher is a vital tool in the research process since this study used a social constructivist philosophical perspective in which knowledge is co-constructed by the researcher and participants through the research process using a qualitative approach

(Costantino, 2008; Creswell & Creswell, 2018; Creswell & Poth, 2017; Glesne, 2016; Merriam & Tisdell, 2016). A qualitative researcher is critical in collecting and analyzing data throughout the study process. A researcher cannot be "a neutral or totally value-free expert" (Charmaz, 2014). Hence, I could not totally detach myself from this study's data collection and analysis process; therefore, I took "a reflexive position" when working on this research project (Charmaz, 2014). I understood that the research method has the potential to influence and be influenced by me (Merriam & Tisdell, 2016). I am a male Chinese American (first-generation immigrant) with an educational and career background in engineering and previous experiences as a Christian entrepreneur in Hong Kong in the field of urban farming. I realize that my biases as a non-native US Midwestern farmer might impact the quality of communications in understanding the culture of the heartland of America. My urban preconceptions might influence how my participants see me as a researcher in a rural context. My special interests in the research topic might not be compatible with those of the prospective participants. My prejudices based on the Protestant Christian faith tradition and Asian American culture might influence the orientation of the conversations. Therefore, rather than being an objective researcher, I acknowledged my stance and prejudices throughout the study, which could improve, on the other hand, the trustworthiness of my findings.

In addition to maintaining reflexivity, it is recommended that qualitative researchers engage in the practice of bracketing. Bracketing is a method that emphasizes the significance of the participants, with the aim of preventing the researcher from imposing their own personal beliefs (Creswell, 2013). To establish appropriate boundaries, I employed both verbal and non-verbal communication strategies to convey several key messages to the study participants. Firstly, I conveyed my role as an engaged listener, demonstrating attentiveness and receptiveness. Secondly, I emphasized my purpose of attentively listening to their narratives, underscoring the significance of their stories. Thirdly, I conveyed the importance and value of the meanings embedded within their narratives, highlighting their relevance to the study. Lastly, I made it clear that my personal educational, faith, and cultural background should not be perceived as exerting any influence on their storytelling process.

Summary of Methodology

The present qualitative study utilized a research design that incorporated a philosophical paradigm of social constructivism and a research approach of basic qualitative research. This choice was based on the alignment with the research question, the researcher's own personal experiences, and the characteristics of the study participants in the rural context of the US Midwest. The data were obtained by several methods, including field observations, one-on-one interviews, and study of archival documents, throughout the state of Iowa, United States of America. The data analysis in this study was conducted using Dedoose, a computer software, which facilitated the application of thematic coding.

The research's trustworthiness was established by employing rigorous methods such as thorough engagement in data, triangulation, and researcher reflexivity to enhance credibility. Additionally, thick description, data saturation, and theoretical grounding are utilized to promote transferability. Moreover, dependability is ensured through prolonged engagement, consistent observation, and examination of discrepant data. Lastly, confirmability is enhanced through member checking, audit trail, and peer review. Ethical considerations were duly acknowledged through adherence to the prescribed rules and regulations set forth by the pertinent organizations, specifically emphasizing the imperative of ensuring the well-being and nonmaleficence of the human subjects concerned. Instead of presenting myself as an impartial researcher, I acknowledge my personal prejudices and preconceived notions throughout the study, potentially enhancing the trustworthiness of my research.

Chapter 4

The Study Context

This chapter provides a comprehensive context of the 33 study participants who were involved in the 14 businesses. Among the 33 informants, 16 were business owners, while the remaining 17 were stakeholders other than owners. Nine of the 14 enterprises were farms, with the remaining five being small businesses other than farms. The purpose of this chapter is to establish a solid foundation for understanding the subsequent findings and to provide a representative narrative that encompasses all participants in this dissertation. It is important to note that while this chapter is crucial for comprehending the findings, it does not constitute part of the findings. The information about these businesses was primarily obtained through the one-on-one interviews with the 33 informants, the observations made during the visits to the 14 research sites with the field notes taken during or right after each visit, and available media sources.

The field notes included the researcher's judgments and views on what had been observed, as well as a wide range of information, such as what was seen, heard, felt, and thought during the field observations. They document my sensory and cognitive experiences in the field. I frequently referred to my field notes for a thorough account of what I witnessed. Observation notes were the first point of contact with the data to be evaluated. They were an essential resource for comprehending the context, nuances, and complexities of the research situation.

Background of Participants

The current study included 33 participants who participated in individual interviews. In terms of gender, there were 20 men and 13 women. The participants' ages were distributed as follows: nine were between the ages of 18 and 35, 13 were between the ages of 36 and 65, and 11 were over the age of 65.

The study participants represented a wide spectrum of business stakeholders. 10 of the participants were farm owners and/or farmers, eight were small business owners other than farms, six were farm workers, four were employees of small businesses, three were customers of small business, one was a community church pastor, and one was an agricultural researcher.

The informants' occupations were likewise diverse. Nine of the participants were farmers, eight were college students, three were farm workers, three were businesswomen, three were college professors, two were church pastors, one was a psychologist, and one was a regional airline pilot. Certain people have dual vocations, such as pastor and farmer, professor and farmer, accountant and farmer, researcher and farmer, professor and businessperson, and so on. Dual vocational participants were mostly part-time or weekend farmers/businessperson. This phenomenon demonstrated the long-lasting impact of farming on the psychological development and internal dynamics of people living in the rural Midwest region of the United States.

Finally, the study participants represented a wide range of faith traditions and affiliations. There were nine Evangelicals, four Quakers, three Catholics, three Baptists, two Presbyterians, two Mennonite/Amish, two Agnostic, one Alliance, one Lutheran, one Puritan, one Methodist, one Mormon, one Unitarian Universalist, and one Hindu. This sample demonstrated one of the key reasons that people immigrated to the United States:

the pursuit of religious freedom, which is a fundamental aspect of the nation's constitutional heritage.

The sample's distribution reflects the cultural diversity and social environment of the Midwestern United States. Table 3 provides a summary of the background information pertaining to the total of 33 study participants.

Background of Businesses

This study involved 14 businesses that were visited. The study participants interviewed in each business type were as follows: 10 from grain farms (corn and soybean), nine from community farms (vegetables and fruits), two from a flower farm, two from a horse farm, three from a salon, two from a real estate business, two from a logistics company, one from an apparel & wardrobe architect business, and one from a medical informatics tech-startup.

The sample's distribution was indicative of the varied business landscape and ecological makeup of the rural Midwestern region in the

United States. Table 4 provides a concise summary of the background information pertaining to a total of 14 participating businesses.

Catholic Worker Community Farm

The primary objective of the Catholic Worker Community Farm was to cultivate an inclusive community that facilitates the cultivation and consumption of nutritious, delectable, and locally sourced sustenance. The farm functioned within the framework of the Catholic Worker movement, a socially conscious movement that embraced individuals from many origins, spiritual orientations, genders, and sexual orientations (Zwick, 2005).

The Catholic Worker Community Farm was situated in Iowa. The farm represented a dynamic and inclusive community consisting of farmers, interns, volunteers, and artists. The farm's fundamental principles centered on sustainable living, a deep sense of care for one's neighbors, and the establishment of a community that actively promoted inclusivity. A study participant initiated the establishment of the farm identified as Mary and her spouse, who opted to register it as a farm entity rather than a non-profit organization. Since its inception in 2008, the organization has demonstrated consistent financial sustainability for over a decade. The farm adhered to sustainable practices and a simple living concept. The farm placed a high emphasis on using sustainable farming practices in order to reduce its ecological impact. The farm has had a notable influence on the nearby community by providing locally sourced food and promoting community engagement in sustainable agricultural practices.

As the researcher, I spent three hours per week on average at the farm during the 2023 growing season (spring to fall) in order to conduct a prolonged observation. Instead of receiving monetary compensation, farm workers were remunerated by food and shelter or a box of fresh farm produce. During my time on the farm, I conducted individual interviews with the founder and seven other farm workers.

Donald Kevin Jason Family Farm

Donald Kevin Jason Family Farm in Iowa was a large-scale, privately owned and managed agricultural enterprise. The primary focus of this farm was the cultivation of maize and soybeans. Donald, the progenitor, was the paternal figure with three offspring. Kevin, one of Donald's children, had a total of nine children of his own. Jason is the eldest son of Kevin. Donald had a total of 16 grandchildren and 11 great-grandchildren. All individuals on the maternal lineage of Kevin originated from Norway due to the unfavorable agricultural conditions prevailing in that region. All individuals on the paternal lineage migrated from Germany to the United States in pursuit of religious liberty. Initially, their intention was to proceed in a westerly direction. Upon their arrival in Iowa, it was discovered that the agricultural soil in this region exhibited a high degree of fertility. Nevertheless, living proved to be hard due to the cold temperatures experienced during the winter season, necessitating the utilization of corn cobs as a means to generate heat and provide warmth amidst the snowy conditions. Ultimately, the ancestors of Kevin established their residence in Iowa during the early 20th century, possessing a substantial 168-acre farmland. In 1906, they constructed their very first barn on the present-day site of the Donald Kevin Jason Family Farm.

William Conservation Farm

William Conservation Farm was a small-scale, privately owned agricultural establishment in Iowa. The William family had maintained ownership of the farm for a period exceeding 130 years. At the time of this study, the farm was under the ownership of the William family and was rented and farmed by the Daniel family, a farmer who had cultivated the land for two successive generations. William held a position of emeritus professor at a university located in Minnesota, the United States.

The William Conservation Farm was an establishment dedicated to sustainable agriculture, employing a diverse range of conservation measures aimed at safeguarding water and soil resources. The aforementioned approaches included cover cropping, crop rotation, reduced tillage, contour farming, terracing, and windbreaks. These approaches have been found to effectively mitigate soil erosion, enhance water quality, and promote biodiversity.

The conservation measures implemented by William Conservation Farm were driven by a commitment to the principles of Quakerism, which emphasized responsible care of the land. According to the perspective of William, it was argued that those who identify as Quakers bear a moral obligation to attend to the well-being of the environment, striving to enhance its condition rather than merely maintaining it at its initial state. The farm additionally endeavored to achieve sustainability in its financial, spiritual, social, and ecological aspects.

Thomas Community Farm

The Thomas Community Farm, located in Iowa, is a small-scale agricultural establishment that demonstrated a steadfast dedication to the principles of sustainable farming. Thomas actively participated with the local farming community. In addition to his role as a research geneticist specializing in plant genetics at the United States Department of Agriculture (USDA), he also held a professorship at a nearby institution, where his research focused on corn insects and crop genetics. His principal focus was on the study of legume crops, such as soybean, peanut, lentil, and other related species. His work aimed to facilitate the availability of integrated genetic and genomic data, thereby empowering researchers and plant breeders in their efforts to enhance the quality of legume crops through the development of improved varieties.

Thomas's faith first aligned with the Mormon tradition and had since transitioned to the Quaker tradition. Thomas engaged in the expression of his faith by actively participating in the preservation of seed diversity. He held the conviction that each seed possesses a sacred quality and extended this belief to encompass the inherent sanctity of all living beings and elements of the creation.

David and Barbara Flower Farm

Following a four-decade tenure as a public school administrator and educator,

David made the decision to retire from his professional pursuits in the field of education. Subsequently, he embarked on a new venture alongside his spouse, Barbara, by establishing a cut flower business. David and Barbara allocated three acres of farmland from their small-scale farm specifically for the Iowa Conservation Reserve Program. The initiative's objective was to incentivize individuals to cease agricultural activities on marginal farmlands and instead designate these properties to protect the Iowan native prairie. The other portion of the agricultural area was allocated for cultivating a diverse range of flowers, including roses, lilies, sunflowers, and dahlias. The cut flowers were afterward marketed and sold in nearby farmers' markets. David and Barbara expressed their satisfaction in delivering aesthetic pleasure and happiness to their clientele while also emphasizing their commitment to positively impacting the local community and the environment at large.

David and Barbara, adherents of the Quaker faith tradition, constructed a temple gate in the vicinity of their flower garden. This gate served as a symbolic representation, signifying that the act of entering the garden embodied not solely the cultivation of flowers but also the cultivation of one's spirituality and simplicity.

Joshua and Donna Logistics

The informants named Joshua and Donna, are a couple, having been raised within a rural Amish community situated in Iowa. Joshua and Donna had a family heritage of farming. Despite having successfully created their own logistics business, the informants in question continued to reside on a farm where they leased most of the farmland to others to farm and use a small piece of farmland to grow more than 200 dozen sweet corn every year for a nearby prison. This agricultural endeavor served as a Christian outreach ministry, providing free sweet corn to prisoners. Joshua and Donna received assistance from local law enforcement personnel who volunteered their personal vacation time to demonstrate their love and care for the smallest brothers in the community.

Karen Family Farm

The informant, Karen, a resident of Iowa, was a multifaceted individual engaged in farmland ownership, urban farming, authorship, photography, videography, and land stewardship. Karen possessed ancestral agricultural land in the northwestern region of Iowa, which coincided with her upbringing on a farm in the same area. In 2011, she made a charitable contribution of 60 acres of her land to the Iowa Natural Heritage Foundation while concurrently engaging in organic farming practices on the remaining portion of her farmland. In recognition of her endeavors to safeguard and enhance her farm, she was bestowed with the Farmland Owner Award by Practical Farmers of Iowa in 2013. In addition, she had authored a publication exploring the historical and cultural aspects of her rural locality. She also created multiple video productions encompassing a range of subjects pertaining to her personal experiences and areas of fascination.

Karen completed her undergraduate studies at a university in Iowa, followed by her graduate studies at a university in Wisconsin and a Christian theological seminary in California. After completing her theological studies in the late 1980s, she resided in northern California, where she experienced an internal prompting to return to her homeland. Upon her arrival in Iowa in 1993, the residence of her grandparents had been completely destroyed by a fire, leaving just a surviving apple tree. Subsequently, the informant proceeded to relocate the apple tree to a college town situated in Central Iowa, where she lived at the time of the interview. In order to foster connections among international students and facilitate their engagement with nature. Karen made the deliberate decision to establish an urban farm in the town to connect people through gardening.

Paul Family Farm

The Paul Family Farm was a medium-scale modest agricultural establishment situated in Eastern Iowa, which was owned and operated by a single-family unit. The establishment was owned and managed by Paul, his spouse, and their three children in conjunction with his parents. The agricultural land cultivated a diverse range of crops, encompassing maize, soybeans, and hay. They also owned three hog houses with 1,200 heads of hogs in each hog house.

Paul demonstrated a strong commitment to Christianity and effectively incorporated his Christian faith into his agricultural practices. He held the belief that agriculture serves as a steward of the land, assuming the responsibility to exercise creation care in its preservation and management. He employed sustainable agricultural methods whenever feasible and demonstrated steadfast dedication to generating high-quality food products without causing detrimental effects to the ecosystem. In addition, he perceived his farm as a means of witnessing his Christian faith to others. Frequently, he extended invitations to anyone to visit his farm, to acquire knowledge about the field of agriculture and observe firsthand the influence of his Christian faith on farming.

The financial sustainability of Paul's Family Farm was achieved through a dual revenue stream consisting of crop sales and a small online business. In addition, Paul had a position as a pastor at a nearby church. Nevertheless, he refrained from receiving financial compensation from the church, as he perceived his pastor role as a gift from God to serve. Paul Family Farm demonstrated social sustainability by fostering strong connections with the surrounding community. From an ecological perspective, Paul Family Farm determined sustainability by implementing sustainable farming practices contributing to the preservation of soil and water quality while also mitigating erosion.

The corporate culture of Paul Family Farm was deeply rooted in Christian values. The family had a strong dedication to diligent effort, integrity, and the equitable treatment of others as an intergenerational family heritage in faith, farming, and business.

Brian Family Farm

Brian's grandfather was engaged in farming. Brian's father, who grew up on a farm, pursued his study until he obtained a Ph.D. degree in statistics. Subsequently, Brian's father embarked on a career at the United States Department of Agriculture (USDA) in

Washington, DC. However, he eventually felt compelled to return to his agricultural roots.

In the 1970s, Brian's father secured an employment at the National Animal Disease

Laboratory located in Iowa. Concurrently, he was able to engage in farming on a nearby 80-acre farmland. Brian also engaged in farm activities on the farm alongside his father in his childhood.

During the 1980s, Brian pursued higher education and obtained a degree in accounting. Subsequently, he worked for the government in Iowa, where he dedicated a significant portion of his professional career. During the 1980s farm crisis in Iowa, Brian utilized his financial expertise to assist his father in navigating the difficulties, afterwards dedicating his vacation time to engage in farming. He emulated his father's career path by pursuing a dual vocation in farming and numbers.

Robert and Sarah Horse Farm

Robert & Sarah Horse Farm was a horse boarding facility situated in Iowa, that is owned and maintained by the Robert and Sarah family, who had extensive experience and involvement in the equine sector spanning a period of more than two decades. The horse farm was equipped with a total of 20 enclosures designated for horsey accommodation. The farm provided wide-ranging boarding choices, including full-care and self-care arrangements, horse-riding instruction, training services, and horse sales. In addition to its primary equine operations, the farm boasted a spacious indoor arena, an extensive outdoor arena, and convenient access to nearby trails. The farm facilitated several activities, including clinics, shows, and camps. The residents in the surrounding area were enthusiastic about disseminating the happiness derived from their devotion to Jesus and horses. The Robert and Sarah family demonstrated the integration of their Christian faith with their business venture through a range of practices. These included engaging in prayer for both their clients and staff, Bible verses sharing after each horse-riding lesson, Bible study groups with students and their parents respectively, fostering an inclusive and secure atmosphere for individuals from diverse backgrounds, and exhibiting responsible and conscientious stewardship towards the environment and animal welfare. The Robert & Sarah Horse Farm offers more than mere horse boarding and horse-riding instruction services; it provided an opportunity to encounter the profound affection and elegance of the glory of God via the splendor and marvels of His handiwork.

Joseph Medinformatics

Joseph was a professor at a university in Iowa. His research interests were in the realm of medical informatics. Additionally, he held the position of president and chief executive officer for Joseph Medinformatics, a technology firm specializing in the research and development of software for medical imaging and video processing technologies.

The Joseph Medinformatics was established in the year 2009 by Professor Joseph and three other partners. The primary offering of the company revolved around a software system designed to analyze recordings obtained from colonoscopy procedures. This system was specifically developed to generate quality measurements and deliver constructive input to gastroenterologists. The firm employed artificial intelligence and computer vision methodologies to identify polyps, quantify withdrawal duration, and evaluate the adequacy of bowel preparation. The primary objective of the program was to enhance the precision and efficacy of colon cancer screening and preventive measures.

Professor Joseph and his colleagues were dedicated to the integration of their Christian faith with their business enterprise. The individuals held the belief that their work served as a means of worshiping and showing reverence towards God, while also acknowledging and appreciating the world He has created. The business endeavored to maintain ethical and professional norms in its research and development activities, as well as in its engagements with stakeholders. The individuals strived to fulfill their responsibility as caretakers of the resources and abilities bestowed upon them by God.

Elizabeth Tailor

Elizabeth Tailor was a small business in Iowa with a flexible workforce of two to five employees over varying seasons. Its business was a comprehensive tailor and bespoke design studio that provided diverse services with tailoring, mending, repair, and the creation of personalized clothing designs. The business was renowned for its dedication to the integration of business practices with the Christian faith. The proprietor of Elizabeth Tailor, known as Elizabeth, has effectively integrated her Christian faith into the core values and operations of her enterprise. The activities of the shop were led by a robust Christian faith that served as the foundation for its mission and values. Elizabeth had a commendable approach towards her employees by always treating them with respect and fairness, thereby establishing a conducive and optimistic work atmosphere. Elizabeth Tailor's principal focus was on achieving financial sustainability, so guaranteeing the longterm viability and profitability of the enterprise. In conjunction with its commitment to financial sustainability, the business also prioritized spiritual sustainability, aiming to cultivate an atmosphere fostering the spiritual welfare of its employees and clientele. Social sustainability is an additional fundamental principle underpinning Elizabeth Tailor's ethos. The establishment actively participated in community engagement and contributed to the growth and development of the local community. In addition, Elizabeth Tailor demonstrated its dedication to ecological sustainability by providing tailoring and repair services, which encouraged the reuse and repurposing of clothing articles. The organizational culture at Elizabeth Tailor was distinguished by its emphasis on creativity, craftsmanship, and meticulousness. The individuals at Elizabeth Tailor exhibited a profound dedication to their craft and demonstrated a strong commitment to providing clients with exceptional products and services of superior quality. Elizabeth Tailor had a substantial influence on both the local community and the global community due to its commitment to excellence and active participation with the community in a "slow fashion."

Deborah Salon

Deborah was someone who belonged to the first generation of immigrants originating from Southeast Asia. The informant's spouse was a farmer in the state of Iowa. Deborah Salon was established four decades ago in Iowa. Deborah exemplified her

Christian faith by caring for people's souls while caring for their tousle, with the intention of fostering their engagement with the church, particularly among newly arrived individuals from Asia. She endorsed business as ministry using her salon business and church leadership experience, following Priscilla and Aquila's tentmaking model mentioned in Chapter 18 of the Book of Acts in the Bible. But other times, Deborah also saw other people doing ministry as a business, with church ministry serving as a platform for someone's business benefit, similar to the business activities described in the Book of

Matthew 21:12 in Scripture.

James Real Estate

James possessed a doctoral degree and had a position as a college administrator in Iowa. In 2011, shortly following the 2008 financial crisis in the United States, the informant's work unit underwent closure, resulting in the termination of his employment at the institution. In light of the challenging circumstances, the informant made the strategic decision to allocate resources towards real estate investment and assumed the role of property manager for a select number of residential properties, so embarking onto a secondary professional pursuit. In his capacity as a landlord, James perceived himself not as a superior figure, but rather as a humble servant dedicated to the welfare of widows and orphans, adhering to the principles espoused by Jesus Christ. He consistently demonstrated compassion towards tenants who were experiencing financial hardships, mirroring the compassionate nature of Jesus, showing mercy towards individuals who were vulnerable and marginalized.

Summary of the Study Context

For the purposes of this study, study participants were chosen from a sample of 14 enterprises, including farms and small businesses located in the rural Midwestern region, primarily in the state of Iowa within the United States. None of the 14 enterprises possessed tax-exempt or charitable non-profit status; rather, they operated as financially selfsustaining entities. The potential benefit that these organizations may derive might not necessarily be in the form of financial returns but rather in the form of reciprocal labor exchanges. The remuneration received by the workers in these organizations might not encompass monetary compensation but non-monetary forms such as provisions for food and shelter, as well as psychological and spiritual benefits.

To gather instances that were rich in information and involved a variety of business and faith traditions, I conducted visits to research sites representing different sorts of businesses, participated in meetings associated with various faith traditions, and extended the duration of my interactions with participants in the field. I interviewed a total of 33 study participants, and observations were made on 14 research sites. The study encompassed a diverse range of businesses, consisting of nine distinct categories of business, and involved informants from ten varied occupational backgrounds and fifteen different faith traditions.

Chapter 4 thoroughly examined the study context of research sites and participants in this study and the underlying justification for the chosen research approach. The findings of this study will be presented in Chapter 5.

Chapter 5

Findings

This basic qualitative study aimed to understand how the business as ministry stakeholders in the rural Midwestern United States practiced and perceived business as ministry for the common good. The current chapter elucidates the findings derived from the conducted study. This study's fieldwork began with observations and one-on-one interviews with 33 research participants from 14 businesses, including nine farms and five small businesses other than farms. The data, which included interview transcripts, field notes, reflective memoranda, and archive materials, were processed using Dedoose, a computer-aided qualitative data analysis software. In Dedoose's terms, 250 codes were generated from 680 excerpts (incidents or "trees" as specified in Chapter 3) with 1,535 code applications, comprising initial codes and focused codes (defined in Chapter 3). These 250 codes were then characterized into 16 categories. As the primary finding of this study, four themes (the "forest" described in Chapter 3) emerged.

Table 5 comprehensively compiles the major themes, categories, and codes. Each theme aligned with a distinct yet complementary and interconnected area of inquiry concerning the participants' practices and perceptions of the financial, spiritual, social, and intellectual aspects of business as ministry for the common good.

Financial Capital—The Financial Aspects

What makes a business valuable financially is the good it does for the glory of God and wealth generation. Through thematic coding, the key categories that came together to form the theme of financial capital were profit, cash, debt, and assets.

Profit—The Lifeblood of Business

Profit is generally the monetary gain generated by a business through the sale of products or services. Profit can be determined by subtracting the total expenses from total revenue. In alternative terms, profit denotes the residual capital of a business after the settlement of all expenditures. Focus coding on the following codes led to the establishment of the "profit" category in this study: "profit is a thing but not everything," "I don't have to be rich to have a comfortable life," "profitable but not exploitative," "for the future generations to profit," and "long-term versus short-term."

"Profit Is a Thing but Not Everything."

Donald, the leader of the Donald Kevin Jason Family Farm, had financially supported overseas missionaries in Africa and Hong Kong his whole life. During the 1980s Midwest farm crisis, his family farm experienced tremendous financial difficulties. One day, when the bankers came to him, Donald recalled during an interview:

> Yeah, when the bankers came down to our family financials and said, "You don't need to spend that money for missions. Just cut that out." I said, "No, I'm not cutting that out." I had to argue about it. It's been at the budget for so many years. The average banker doesn't understand this. They think that's just an item of expenses, and it's just throwing money down the drain. The missionary budget has not been included

in calculating the farm's profit. No. I've never had to call missionaries and say I can't support you this year. It was a blessing that God gave me to give back the glory to God through sharing it with missionaries in need. No, I'm not gonna cut it out.

The "average banker" and a faithful farmer had different formulas for

calculating profit. Moreover, study participants Joshua, Donna, and Paul also

did not agree with the

"average banker" in the calculation of business profit. They agreed with

Donald that an element of Christian faith must be in the formula.

During an interview with Kevin, a son of Donald, I asked a similar question,

"Kevin, you're not only consistently providing financial support to your

church ministries but also gave ten years of your life for missions abroad.

Don't you think those are expenses of your financial book or your career as a

professional farmer?" He explained his rationale to me:

> Financial is still a hard issue. It's just hard for people to give. When I understand what I have, I think I have a gift of giving that God has put in my life even since I was a little kid. I've always enjoyed giving stuff away better than getting stuff. That's just something that I don't know where I could think about it. We have a family tradition to set up a giving account. In January, we fill the account with the whole year's budget. If we had a good year, we would give more. Profit is a thing, but not everything.

"What if there was a bad year?" I spontaneously asked.

> Well, if it was a bad year, we always hope that the next year, the Lord will take good care of us in his providence." While working at the mission agency for fundraising projects, I worked with many large donors. They had their castle of a house and got those luxury cars in the driveway. When we asked for a donation, they said, "Money doesn't grow on trees." I don't know where I got that. So, having a lot doesn't necessarily translate into a lot.

The "average rich" and faithful missionary farmer had different priorities for profit.

"I Don't Have to Be Rich to Have a Comfortable Life."

Elizabeth Tailor's proprietor, Elizabeth, positioned her business in direct opposition to the trendy fast fashion business. She narrated her story in an interview:

> I began my college studies at a local institution in Iowa, majoring in biology. I was going into medicine. I wanted to study medicine with the goal of helping people. In college, I got the opportunity to study more about the fashion industry, and I've always had a talent for creating and sewing. And I made a buddy, a woman who ran a fair-trade business in Southeast Asia. She was making a positive difference by providing jobs in a country with a scarcity of fair jobs. I watched how she helped people by channeling her natural aptitude toward one thing or another. She did not consider herself a missionary. She thought of herself as a Christian who ran a business and was involved in the community. I observed how she used her business as a mission. That changed my view about how I could utilize business to further God's mission. So, I went with her. Later, I changed my college major.

I followed up on her thought by asking, "Do you believe your family heritage influenced your career path?" Elizabeth continued:

> Both my maternal and paternal grandparents were farmers. My mom was a nutritionist. My dad is a pastor. My mother is a first-generation Christian; my father is a second-generation Christian. I'd always believed I'd be a missionary. I'll become a doctor. My family has always been supportive of whatever I wanted to achieve. And I was raised to believe that you are a believer no matter where you are. The church assumed that missionaries should go to a mission field and teach the gospel to people in villages who had never heard of Jesus before, but I had some ideas about it. Mmm-hmm, being a missionary in quotes about traveling to another country was better or the best. Christians do that. But I needed to demolish some of those ideologies. Yeah. I am confident that my family's heritage had an impact on me. They believed in my ability to build a business that would glorify God.

> In my business, I don't care about popular brands or trends. I'm more concerned with sustainability and fair trade, lowering my carbon footprint, and educating others about what it means to buy something

and then discard it a few months later. I dislike the concept of constantly needing to buy brand-new items. I enjoy tailoring and modifications. You modify things when they fit well. I'm doing something that may not generate a lot of profit. But I enjoy what I do. That's why I feel safe. I don't need to be rich to have a comfortable life.

The "average fast fashion player" and a faithful businesswoman had different tastes in fashion and perceptions of profit, i.e., maximizing versus sustainable.

"Profitable but Not Exploitative."

The study participant, David, had chosen to retire from his professional endeavors in education after serving as a public-school administrator and educator for forty years. The individual undertook a new entrepreneurial endeavor in collaboration with his wife, Barbara, by establishing a cut flower business. A fraction of their 11-acre property was allocated for cultivating various flowers, such as roses, lilies, sunflowers, and dahlias. Subsequently, these cut flowers were commercially promoted and retailed in nearby farmers' markets. David defined himself as follows:

> I am a Quaker. As I understand the history of Quakers, Quakers were often successful businesspeople. One of the Quaker values was honesty. That is doing business in a way that is profitable but not exploitative. If you do business with a Quaker, you can trust that they will be fair and honest in their business, and they were very successful in many ways. So, in Pennsylvania, there was a Quaker community originally founded by William Penn, and many Quaker families became quite successful in business because they were trusted in their business relations.

David went on to relate Quakers' businesses to the community:

> The Quaker values are to profit, not in a way that is unfair or harmful to others. So, I think my wife and I are very concerned about climate change and its environmental effects. I think a lot of that comes from

people's businesses focusing only on short-term profit without considering the long-term impacts of things that they might do in businesses or some things like pollution that are so bad. So, chronic, real problems are growing out of humans being greedy or at least having a very short-term focus.

Profitable but not exploitative was the principle of Quaker business. James and

Deborah, study participants, agreed with David and saw "profitable but not exploitative" as Christian ideals of business as ministry by freezing their rates or rents for those customers in financial difficulty.

For the Future Generations to Profit

In an interview with William, the William Conservation Farm proprietor, on the topic of motivation to conserve the water and soil at his farm, he expressed his passion for what he had been doing by stating, "As a Quaker, I care about the good of not only our generation but also the generations to come." Participants in the study Robert, Sarah, Paul, Karen, Joshua, and Donna all agreed with William when he said, "I care about the good of not only our generation but also the generations to come."

Long-Term Versus Short-Term

David and Barbara were a couple in this study. In an interview, they shared their perspectives about-long term and short-term considerations. Barbara said,

> After we retired, we bought 11 acres of farmland. We used part of it to grow flowers, such as roses, lilies, sunflowers, and dahlias for our cut flowers business in nearby farmers' markets. Although it's still in the start-up phase, we believe that our business will be profitable. And yet, we consider the profit as our shortterm goal.

David said,

We dedicated seven acres of farmland to Iowa Conservation Reserve Program as a conservation reserve wetland to grow native prairie and Iowa plants. We get a small amount of income every year for having the land in that reserve program from the USDA. The program is to encourage people to take what is marginal farmland out of production. So, it's not growing corn or soybeans. If you're willing to do that with some of your land, then the government will give you some money every year for doing that. It mostly has a lot of big blue stems, a lot of Indian grass, and a lot of various other native Iowa prairie plants. We have been working over the course of the last 15 years or so to establish the prairie plants as a long-term investment.

During a water and soil conservation promotion event at the William Conservation

Farm, Richard, a study participant, offered his thoughts on natural and social

sciences. Richard was a PhD student at a local university studying sustainable

agriculture and biosystems engineering. At William Conservation Farm,

where an experimental engineering system was established, he was doing

research and development on water and soil conservation technology.

Drawing from his knowledge and experience in research, Richard

imparted the following insights:

We can see as many great technical solutions as we can develop in school. And yet, it still takes a lot of human partnership and collaboration to make things happen, especially when we're talking about those kinds of large issues that affect people at such a large scale from regionally to globally, like climate change, water quality, and flooding, all those things. So, there's a need for me going on not just as technical expertise to solve problems; having the ability to work with others, or maybe often different from you, who have a different background than you with slightly different ways of doing things but figuring out a way to collaborate. Collaboration makes solutions happen.

In connection with his practical involvement with farm owners and

farmers in the execution of his research project, Richard described his

encounters:

I believe there is a limit to what our technical engineering solutions can accomplish without human collaboration. Daniel, the farmer who rents farmlands from multiple farm owners, taught me that some farm owners consistently care about the land's conservation, while others only care about the rent they receive from farmers. This is likely a result of their faith traditions about land stewardship. Hmm. That's not the area for engineers to work on.

Richard expressed his philosophical perspective on whether social science education is necessary for engineers:

If the institution could offer interdisciplinary programs such as science and theology integration, technology and anthropology integration, or integration of engineering and psychology, that would be awesome.

The study participants understood that profit is required for a firm to operate in the same way that blood is required for the human body to function. A company cannot pay its obligations, invest in new prospects, or grow if it does not make a profit. However, planet Earth cannot be sustained if businesspeople are only concerned with profit.

Debt—A Financial Leverage

Debts are the monetary obligations of a business to its creditors. A financial obligation, usually accompanied by interest, that necessitates repayment. Borrowing money, issuing bonds, or utilizing credit cards are all methods by which organizations may accumulate debt. The "debt" category was established in this research by employing focus coding on the following codes: "land, debt, and faith," "leverage in faith for courage," and "zero interest loans."

Land, Debt, and Faith

The person identified as Donald served as the patriarch of the Donald Kevin Jason Family Farm. Presently, Donald has three children, sixteen grandchildren, and eleven greatgrandchildren. Kevin was a son of Donald, and Jason was a son of Kevin. The farm encompassed over 4,000 acres of arable land, using cutting-edge agricultural technologies such as GPS-enabled automated farm machinery such as the John Deere autopilot planter Kevin and the autopilot combined. Donald expressed his gratitude, stating:

> I'm so blessed. I have a very blessed life and a very blessed family. In history,
> Iowa saw the most severe impact during the farm crisis of the 1980s in the Midwest. There were many farmers losing their farmlands. I lost all my land not once but twice! We expanded too fast in the 1980s, and it was going well, and all of a sudden, the farm crisis hit. We went too far, and the leverage in the bank pulled out on me. The guy from the bank said, "Well, if you can come up with this much money to pay off your debt on your land, we will let you go free." I was very close to half of the bankruptcy. I never gave up. I worked hard trying to convince the bank to stay with it. My good friend worked for a guy at a big chemical company. The guy came down to help me negotiate with the bank and pay off my debt. He then rented the land back to me. I gradually expanded the hog house and land ownership. So, we were back. Four years later, the same thing happened again. Hogs' price was down in cents. I lost all the land.
>
> When a big farmer in Eastern Iowa lost all his land to the bank, he killed two people in the bank, killed his wife at home, and shot himself. He didn't have faith. The world was really coming to him. That was a really sad time. During the farm crisis in the 1980s, farmers went into depression and even killed the bankers who took the land from the farmers for their own profit. You know, land is a part of our lives.
>
> For me, there came the same lawyer again. She worked things out. Now, my debts have been paying off enough. So, I think I'm financially better off today. That's all due to my faith in God. Yeah. God will bring the right people in my path. God saved me and saved my family.

The land is an identity of farmers. Debt could be a leverage or a killer. Faith could save one's life. Informants Robert and Sarah, Paul, Karen, and William all agreed with Donald when he mentioned that land is a farmer's identity debt may be both a source of leverage and a source of detrimental force.

Leverage in Faith for Courage

The informant, known as Brian, shared his story:

I have worked as an accountant for the Iowa government since I graduated with an accounting degree. Five years ago, I retired in my mid-50s and had been working as a full-time farmer on our family farm. My grandfather was a dairy farmer in Illinois. My father, who grew up on a farm, pursued his studies until he obtained a Ph.D. degree in statistics. Subsequently, my father began a career at the United States Department of Agriculture (USDA) in Washington, DC. However, my father eventually felt compelled to return to his agricultural roots. In the 1970s, Brian's father secured employment at a national research facility located in Iowa. Concurrently, he engaged in farming on an 80-acre property nearby, retired from his government job, and became a full-time farmer at 56.

It was difficult for our farm during the 1980s farm crisis here in Iowa. My dad might have run into negative equity in his balance sheet. I had just graduated from college and got a loan to buy a larger tractor for my father. Yeah, it was the first loan in my life. Praise God: we survived because of that leverage.

Leverage in debt for business, leverage in faith for courage. Business is characterized as a risk-taking endeavor.

Zero Interest Loans

The Catholic Worker Community Farm was registered as a farm entity rather than a tax-exempted non-profit or charity organization. The founding couple were the owners of this 11-acre farm. And yet the vision and mission of the farm were voluntary simplicity and voluntary poverty. In questions of the farm ownership, Mary, one of the owners of the farm, shared their founding story:

We first started with a group with the same goal and passion. We were looking for a place to start a farm. We rented one acre here and lived in our neighbor's house for a few months, and then we camped here on the farm for the first year. That was how we started. It went pretty well. So, we rented two acres, and then slowly, we built our house here on the farm, and then we rented three acres. After five years, the landowners were ready to sell the farm to us. With some loans at no interest from other Catholic Worker groups, we could own the farm, including the house we built. It's also a kind of a Catholic Worker value to have no interest on loans, which really helped. We were able to pay back those loans within nine years. So, our goal was to have some cash from our vegetable sales to pay off our loans. During the land purchase, we also got some financial support from friends and our savings for years. We just kind of put many things together to buy that land. Despite the land value going up and down these years, we still live in simplicity willingly.

Microloan with no interest has spiritual value to incubate business as ministry. The study participants understood that debt is a leverage to finance a business's operations or investments as well as a risk.

Cash—The Financial Fuel

The "cash" category was developed using the codes "a long-term optimization," "faith is our energy flow behind the cash flow," and "fresh farm produce as cash." Cash was the financial fuel to drive the business as ministry from its vision and mission to performance and outcome.

A Long-Term Optimization

The study participant, identified as Paul, was raised on a family farm and maintained a dual occupation as both a farmer running his family farm and a pastor serving the local community church. Paul exemplified a compelling instance of integrating profitmaking business and Christian ministry. He appeared to be a financial expert and imparted his practices and perspectives in financial aspects:

Well, with farming, one year blends into the next. Farmers are cash-poor and asset-rich businesspeople. We don't have a lot of cash, but we have a lot of stuff to do with. So, it all gets pumped back into the farm. So, you can't simply do it in a year. It's near the end of summer now. We haven't sold anything that we harvested last fall. We wanted to wait for the right time for a better market price. In the meantime, we must prepare for the coming fall harvest. So, managing cash flow is like a multi-year project assessment. So, we need faith for crops to grow and to manage the farm's cash flow and assets.

A farm's financial management was a long-term aspect. Rather than maximization, it required optimization. It required faith. Informants Robert and Sarah indicated that a long-term cash flow optimization was helpful in the financial stability of their horse farm because they also purchased and sold some horses from time to time.

"Faith Is Our Energy Flow Behind the Cash Flow."

The study participant, Joseph, had the position of professor emeritus specializing in the domain of medical informatics at a university in Iowa. He co-founded Joseph Medinformatics, a technology firm, alongside three other partners who were professors and medical doctors. Joseph shared his experience in financial management of a technology start-up under the incubator of the university:

This is a very difficult but good learning experience because I do not have a family history of starting or doing business. We're a startup company. We do not have a lot of cash to start with. So, starting processes needed some money. We pulled up our time and energy. We wanted to commercialize our research in the university with a startup profit-making company. So, we are applying for a grant from the National Science Foundation to support our research. When we discovered that the technology could help people through colonoscopy, a screening test for colon cancer, we realized that this technology would be very helpful for human beings, not just for medical doctors.

Most of us are researchers. We must learn how to patent the technology. We must learn a business's financial aspects, including marketing, sales, intellectual property application, filing taxes, cash flow management, and talking to the attorney. These are all new to me. With Christian faith in place, I believe we could make it work to glorify God through serving people in the medical field. Faith is our energy flow behind the cash flow.

Fresh Farm Produce as Cash

Lisa was a farm worker at the Catholic Worker Community Farm. She shared her unique experience and perspective:

> Work-for-food has been my job at the farm for three years. I love this program because instead of getting paid money, we get a box of fresh farm veggies and fruits for our work. I'd rather have fresh food than cash because I can connect with my food more directly. I helped plant seedlings, pull weeds, and harvest veggies and fruits at the farm. The fruits and vegetables from the farm were sweeter than those from the grocery stores because we ate them right after they were picked, without going through all the steps. The idea is called "farm-totable." In a psychological sense, I was happy when I ate and shared what I had grown with my family. Because of this, I often took my two boys to work on the farm with me. Kids enjoy being outside and talking to other people.

Farm experience was more valuable than cash.

> The study participants saw cash as analogous to the fuel that propels an automobile.

A car cannot move without fuel. Similarly, a business cannot function without cash.

Assets—The Financial Seeds

The codes "health and peace are my assets," "an exchange between tangible and intangible assets," and "the perceived assets" served as the foundation for the development of the "assets" category. Assets were the financial seeds of business as ministry, a material part of a firm to start up and remain in a sustainable business and ministry.

"Health and Peace Are My Assets."

The study participant, Deborah, operated a relatively high-cash and low-asset salon business and served in several church ministries. In questions about financial aspects of her business and church ministries, Deborah shared her practices and perspectives:

> I used my cash to build a separate account for offering to God. Although my income and offers may be small compared to those of professional or rich people in the church, I've never reduced my offering in the past forty years. God has blessed me with health and peace in my personal life and business. I intentionally separate my business finance from that of my offering to the church. I see my service to God through my business as a gift, giving back to God and sharing with people in the community. I also served God as a decant at the church. I've occasionally seen some cases where people used church ministry as an opportunity for business gain. I think they should be taking advantage of church ministry as their business. It's no good, no good. Sooner or later, once the business with the church became difficult, even just a little bit, they left the church without a solid ground in faith.

Health and peace were Deborah's assets; pleasing God and sharing with people in spiritual need were her cash flow. Business as ministry utilized business as a vehicle for giving back to God and sharing with people in need. Ministry as business was taking advantage of church ministry for business profit.

An Exchange Between Tangible and Intangible Assets

Karen, one of the study participants, shared her insight about tangible and intangible assets:

> Practical Farmers of Iowa educated me on farmland conservation. As a learning outcome, I donated 60 acres of my land to the Iowa Natural Heritage Foundation in 2011. I wanted to convert agricultural practices to organic production to ensure that the land and its natural resources would be conserved for generations to come. I understood that besides

providing resources for the human spirit, the land must also support birds, wildlife, pollinators, and clean water. I did have a trade between tangible and intangible assets because bigger is not better. Small is safe. My land ownership is no less than mercy.

Land has intangible value in addition to its tangible market value.

The Perceived Assets

When I inquired of Joseph about his perspective regarding his

company assets, he replied:

> Our faith and know-how are both assets to our company. We'd see how much money we could make from our know-how if we didn't have faith. When we have know-how and faith together, we ask how many people our expertise can help. After all, both viewpoints could lead to the same business result in terms of money, but the latter would provide us with higher perceived assets.

There were perceived assets. The most valued perceived asset of study

participants Robert and Sarah was witnessing the growth of Christian faith in

their horseback riding instruction students. The study participants understood

that assets are the cornerstone of a firm, just as seeds are the foundation of a

plant. Assets are what enable a company to develop and thrive.

Participants in the study, in brief, were exposed to the significance of

financial capital in the contexts of both business and ministry. They perceived

profit as the lifeblood that sustained both the ministry and business, debt as a

form of financial leverage, cash as the financial fuel, and assets as the

financial seeds.

Spiritual Capital—The Spiritual Aspects

The good a business does for human flourishing and the glory of God

is what gives it spiritual value. The main categories that came together to form the theme of spiritual capital through thematic coding were wisdom, values, culture, and ministry.

Wisdom—The Spiritual Light

The initial codes, "faith, hope, and love—the guiding principles," "empathy and kindness," and "serving the people in need," were the basis for the creation of the "wisdom" category. Wisdom was the spiritual light for business as ministry, just like the sunlight for a plant, an essential and critical element for sustainable growth.

A Picture of the Next Generations

In an interview with William, the William Conservation Farm proprietor, I asked,

"What inspired you to conserve the water and soil at your farm?"

William expressed his passion for what he had been doing by stating, "As a Quaker,

I care about the good of not only our generation but also the generations to come."

According to its public communication on the internet and my field notes, William Conservation Farm was committed to using its agricultural practices and resources to advance the common good in accordance with Christian values in the following ways:

The Farm's mission: The farm's mission statement reads, "To sustainably and ethically provide our community with high-quality food." This declaration emphasized the farm's dedication to its customers and the environment.

Sustainable agricultural practices: The farm employed sustainable agricultural practices that conserve resources and safeguard the environment. This included crop rotation, cover cropping, and integrated pest management practices.

Local food: The farm distributed its produce to local grocery stores and restaurants and directly to consumers at its farm stand. This reduces the environmental impact of food transportation and promotes local economic growth.

Involvement in the community: The farm is actively involved in the local community. Produce is donated to local food pantries and soup kitchens, and educational events on the latest research and development of water and soil conservation technologies are hosted in partnership with local universities, conservation groups, and agricultural engineering firms.

Several informants, including Paul, David, Barbara, Joshua, and Donna, agreed with William when he said, "I care about the good of not only our generation, but also the generations to come."

A Complementary Balance of Natural and Social Sciences

During a water and soil conservation promotion event at the William Conservation Farm, Richard, a study participant, offered his thoughts on natural and social sciences. Richard was a PhD student at a local university studying sustainable agriculture and biosystems engineering. At the William Conservation Farm, where an experimental engineering system was established, he was doing research and development on water and soil conservation technology.

Drawing from his knowledge and experience in research, Richard imparted the following insights:

> We can see as many great technical solutions as we can develop in school. And yet, it still takes a lot of human partnership and collaboration to make things happen, especially when we're talking about those kinds of large issues that affect people at such a large scale from regionally to globally, like climate change, water quality, and flooding, all those things. So, there's a need for me going on not just as technical expertise to solve problems; having the ability to work with others, or maybe often different from you, who have a different background than you with slightly different ways of doing things but figuring out a way to collaborate. Collaboration makes solutions happen.

In connection with his practical involvement with farm owners and farmers in the execution of his research project, Richard described his encounters:

> I believe there is a limit to what our technical engineering solutions can accomplish without human collaboration. Daniel, the farmer who rents farmlands from multiple farm owners, taught me that some farm owners consistently care about the land's conservation, while others only care about the rent they receive from farmers. This is likely a result of their faith traditions about land stewardship. Hmm. That's not the area for engineers to work on.

Richard expressed his philosophical perspective on whether social science education is necessary for engineers:

> If the institution could offer interdisciplinary programs such as science and theology integration, technology and anthropology integration, or integration of engineering and psychology, that would be awesome.

Planet Earth cannot be sustained if profit is the only thing to be concerned with.

Thomas, a participant in the study, expressed his agreement with the integration of both natural and social sciences. His viewpoints were reinforced by his methodical academic background in biology and anthropology.

The Works of Mercy, a Common Good of Faiths

The Catholic Worker Community Farm's mission is to "grow food, community, and hope." This statement stresses the farm's dedication to producing food for the community, developing the community, and giving its stakeholders hope. Patricia, a study participant, was a farm manager of the Catholic Worker Community Farm. She introduced the Works of Mercy as a belief and practice of the farm:

> We are devoted to living the Gospel with a Christlike heart via works of mercy. We grow food and distribute it to local food banks and soup kitchens. We also have a work-for-food program, where people could work on the farm in exchange for a portion of the produce. We provided adult clothing for needy people and temporary shelter for homeless people. We gave fresh produce and other nutritious foods to persons who were ill or had limited access to nutritious foods. We advocated for prisoners' human dignity and organized visits to detained people. In addition, the farm is a safe haven for people of all faiths and ethnicities. We conducted various events and workshops throughout the year to promote social justice and environmental care for sustainable agriculture and community living.

The Catholic Worker Community Farm exemplified what it means to live the works of mercy as a Christian ministry in the twenty-first century. The farm was an inclusive place for individuals of different backgrounds to live harmoniously and care for one another for the common good.

Christopher, a study participant, was an international college student from India with a Hindu religious background. He worked part-time as a farm worker at the Catholic Worker Community Farm during the 2023 growing season. Concerning his distinct perspectives on the Catholic Worker business as a Christian ministry from the standpoint of a Hindu, Christopher

responded,

> No, I never had any conflict over there. Like the farm's mission, my
> faith tradition also speaks about serving humanity.

"Oh, that's a common good of faiths," I realized.

Christopher said,

> Aside from that, I haven't really experienced faith activities explicitly
> at the farm. Like everyone else, I don't think I've ever discussed my
> faith with anyone on the farm. Apart from knowing or hearing about
> the Catholic Worker Movement. I haven't talked to anyone in depth
> about their practice or faith.

"What motivated you to work on the farm then?" I asked.

Christopher responded,

> What motivated people to be involved with the farm was that we didn't
> talk about our faith traditions, even with the leader about how she
> came up with this idea. Instead, we lived out our spiritualities by
> serving one another and the community. One of the leaders has run
> this farm for at least 15 years. I had already spoken with her. We have
> not discussed anyone's faith in depth. So, the only thing we have in
> common is service and selflessness. So that's something I've noticed
> around the farm.

Actions speak louder than words.

The study participants noticed that wisdom shines like a beacon in the

dark, illuminating the path ahead. Wisdom allows a person to see clearly and

make informed decisions.

Values—The Spiritual Roots

The initial codes, "faith, hope, and love—the guiding principles,"

"empathy and kindness," and "serving the people in need" were the basis for

the creation of the "values" category. Christian values were the spiritual roots to support the growth of the spiritual capital of a business as a Christian ministry.

Faith, Hope, and Love—The Guiding Principles

During an interview, the individual, identified as Donald, recounted the challenging events in his life that occurred during the 1980s farm crisis in Iowa:

> In the 1980s, we went way too far. And the bank took back the loan I took out. We really did lose all the land, not once, oh, twice! It was tough for me, yeah, really tough. We now own 4,000 acres of land. We've already paid enough. I believe I'm financially better off now. It's critical to have faith in God.

Kevin, a study participant, was Donald's son. Kevin never lost his excitement for working on the farmland, even putting in fourteen hours daily during planting and harvesting seasons. He talked about how farming was his passion:

> I'm always thinking about how great the harvest is going to be. And if it's a bad harvest, I wonder how great the next year will be. We're always optimistic about what is coming, a hope for seeds breaking through the soil, clouds breaking into rain, and plants growing stronger and larger. There's always hope.

In Kevin's perspective, hope served as a motivating force that enabled him to work 14 hours per day and move the mountain and cross the Death Valley in his life.

Jason, a study participant, was Kevin's son. Jason considered himself both a missionary and a farmer's kid. He stated:

My dad was a missionary for ten years and a farmer for the rest of his life. I'm grateful that Jesus loves me so I could have both experiences as a missionary and farmer's kid. I loved being around my dad, particularly in the machine shop. I loved to organize the shop to increase our work efficiency. Observing and getting to know many farming details was comfortable, especially during the harvest season. I think our family is full of love. I want to continue my parents' legacy, and I'm comfortable being the next generation of our family farm. Love played a crucial role in the succession of ownership and leadership of a family business. In the Donald Kevin Jason Family Farm, faith, hope, and love were regarded as the primary Christian business values for the common good.

Multiple informants, namely Lisa, Patricia, Jennifer, Paul, Anthony, and John have also expressed that faith, hope, and love are the essential Christian principles for operating a business as a ministry for the common good.

Empathy and Kindness

The study participant, identified as James, had a real estate business. He used his business as a means to love and care for those single mothers and their children with flexible payment schedules and sometimes even forgiving their rents. In the long run, he became trustful with his tenant families. During an interview, a study participant named

Edward, a tenant of James, described his business relationship with James:
> I think his real estate business could be a Christian run business. He's not only caring the property but also show mercy to his tenants. I can tell from the comparison to my previous landlord who always told me, "Just pay the rent without delay." I think James made a difference on the community through his Christian characters of showing mercy to others.

In James's business, love served as compassion, allowing him to treat his stakeholders with dignity and empathy and trust that God would provide the means and guidance he needed to secure his company's long-term

viability.

Serving the People in Need

Joshua and Donna, two study participants, were raised in an Amish
village in

Southeastern Iowa. The individuals possessed both a family farm and a

logistics company. During an interview, Joshua recounted an anecdote

concerning the provision of sweetcorn to the smallest brothers in the

community:

> I still remember about seven years ago, a chaplain at the correction
> center, we knew each other very well, came up to us after a church
> Sunday service. He asked us if we could raise sweetcorn for the
> prisoners because they don't get sweetcorn due to the limited budget;
> it takes about 200 dozen at a time for all the prisoners. And we said
> yes, we could do it with no money involved but as a Christian
> ministry. We've been taking sweetcorn to the prison for years now.
> Every time when Donna and I received a thank-you card signed
> by the prisoners, we saw each one of them. Yeah, I mean, yes, they
> made significant mistakes in their lives. They've done things they
> shouldn't have done, and that's why they're in. But they still are
> individuals. They still ... They said, they are missing their families.

"They're so isolated." I echoed.

He continued the story:

> One of the prisoners wrote us, he's been in prison for 30 years but
> have never had sweetcorn before, so thank you so much for the
> sweetcorn. Yeah. It's so touched. That's just something that we take
> for granted. I'm sorry, you can tell my voice sounds different.

"Yes, I could see your tears ...," I responded, "You and Donna are
Christlike

Christians loving and caring for the smallest brothers in the society."

Joshua could not suppress his tears, saying, "Yeah, when you read their words, your heart goes out ..." Joshua and Donna were compassionate in serving the people in need.

The study participants held that values bring stability and nourishment to a person's spiritual life like roots do for a plant. Values are responsible for anchoring a person's beliefs and guiding their behaviors.

Culture—The Spiritual Soil

Based on the initial codes "a legacy," "family heritage in the faith," "fast fashion versus slow fashion," "fast food versus slow food," "fast culture versus slow culture," and "fast faith tradition versus slow faith tradition," the "culture" category was established. Culture was the spiritual soil of business as ministry, on which the spiritual capital of a firm was cultivated.

A Legacy

During an interview, Donald, a participant in the study, recounted the missionary legacy of his family:

> My grandfather administered the family farm as a Christian mission center, accommodating overseas missionaries from Africa and Hong Kong. My sister spent her entire life as a missionary single lady in South America. Kevin, my son, Kevin, had spent ten years of his life as a full-time missionary besides his farming vocation. We have a blessed farm; our lives have been so blessed.

Family Heritage in the Faith

The study participant, identified as Paul, was raised on a family farm and maintained a dual occupation as both a farmer running his family farm and a pastor serving the local community church. Paul exemplified a compelling instance of integrating profitmaking business and Christian ministry. He recounted his church-planting story:

> About 20,000 to 25,000 people live in our county here in Iowa. It is an agricultural county in a remote rural area. Any big city in Iowa is an hour's drive away. It was in 2012 that we planted a community church nearby. From then on, I've been the pastor at this church.

In relation to his gift of preaching and in a response to a question if there was a clergy root in his family tree, Paul responded, "My dad has never been a pastor; he's a farmer. But it wasn't until I became a church pastor that I learned that my grandfather worked as a farmer and a pastor."

It seemed that the phenomenon of transgenerational family heritage pertained to both nature and nurture.

Fast Fashion Versus Slow Fashion

> Elizabeth, the research participant, ran a slow fashion company called Elizabeth

Tailor. "Slow fashion" was a completely foreign concept to me. So, I asked the tailor,

"What is slow fashion?"

> Elizabeth explained slowly:

> To comprehend slow fashion, we must first understand fast fashion. Fast fashion, as a business model, is all about producing a large number of items rapidly and cheaply. Fast fashion businesses frequently imitate the latest looks of celebrities and expensive fashion designers. They then use synthetic textiles and cheap labor to make these fashions fast and cheaply. Customers can be given new styles every few weeks.
>
> When I think about slow fashion, I envision a piece that will last for generations. You will be able to wear it for the next 30 years. I can wear some of my grandmother's stuff because it was well-made and won't break apart after a year. Fast fashion is the polar opposite of slow fashion.

"It appears that fast fashion would make more money than slow fashion. Who will be your returning customer if someone buys some clothing from you and wears them for 30 years? Is your slow fashion venture financially viable?" I appeared to be making good business sense.

> She went on to say:
> Well, the way fast fashion produces big amounts of goods at low prices typically results in a lot of waste, pollution, and labor exploitation. Slow fashion is about being more conscious of what we buy and wear. It's about wearing clothes that are well-made and that we enjoy wearing. It's also about caring for the planet Earth.

> "Wow! That is different, as different as fast food and slow food." I

looked to be gaining a better understanding.

Fast Food Versus Slow Food

> I asked Thomas, a professor and plant geneticist, "What is slow food?"

> "Come with me," Thomas said.

> I went with him to his self-sustaining garden. "Wow! Your garden reminded me of

Eden, and I felt spiritual." I was astounded at the range of plants found in a home garden.

Thomas was overjoyed with his garden yield. "There are apple, pawpaw, peach trees, vegetables, beans, maize, pepper, berries, and other fruit plants. This is a unique soybean. A huge, flat black seed distinguishes it. They have not yet become black. You can just eat it."

"Wow! It's so fresh! I've never tasted soybeans like this before. I got my tofu from the grocery store."

Every experience I had in the garden continued to astonish me.

Thomas continued his illustration of slow food:

> I grow my own food. To prepare my own tofu, I grow the soybeans, cook them, grind them, or press out the milk, and then add coagulants for minutes. Tofu was cheap to buy in the store. But do you realize how much of a carbon footprint the store tofu had? The soybeans would have to be carried from the field to the distribution bins, then to the plant, and finally to the retailers, often across the globe. As a result, fast food has a high carbon footprint, whereas slow food has a low or zero carbon footprint, such as grow-your-own-food and farm-to-table.

Fast Culture Versus Slow Culture

As an experiential thinker, Thomas couldn't stop sharing his thoughts:

> I majored in math and anthropology in college. I wanted to know why individuals acted the way they did. I wrote my master's book on ecological anxiety. I believed that most of us have an innate urge to connect with and relate to things outside of ourselves. That was one of my gardening motivations, I believe. It's my spiritual experience in gardening that allowed me to communicate with one component of nature. When you stop gardening, not just slow down, but stop and notice, you'll have your own silent appreciation, and you'll see that everyone is sacred, everything is holy.

Fast Faith Tradition Versus Slow Faith Tradition

Practicing a slow culture, I kept silent for Thomas to continue:

> I think nature, in general, wants to be diverse, and in an ecosystem, plants, animals, and lives will come to fill all available niches. In general, I believe that maintaining a monoculture involves a lot of energy and some damage. As a result, I believe there is an equilibrium in nature with increased diversity.

"So, as an analogy, can I say there's an equilibrium in human society with increased diversity of faith traditions?" I inquired. Then, there was a silence with appreciation.

The study participants believed that culture provides the conditions for spiritual growth. It is what allows faith to grow and thrive just as soil gives the nutrients for plant growth.

Ministry—A Spiritual Vessel

The "ministry" category was formed in accordance with the initial codes "education as ministry," "YouTube as ministry," "if we live simply, others could simply live," "a connection to the land," and "a safe therapy." Ministry was a spiritual vessel for a Christian to practice business as a Christian ministry. There were ministries inside and outside the firm, both intrinsic and instrumental.

Education as Ministry

John, a study participant, was the lead pastor of a local community church. The church provided a number of ministries to farmers and business owners, including a weekly Bible study for farmers, a monthly business networking group, and a mentorship program for young entrepreneurs. This church was home church to three research participants, i.e., two farmers, one business owner, and two farm workers. During an interview with John, he responded:

> I'm not quite familiar with the term business as ministry. I don't think we've talked about that very much as a church. We usually talked about how to be a good neighbor with biblical principles of humility, service, and love. We also talked about a servant-hearted business practice that treats people well and with respect. We have church ministry for overseas short-term and long-term missions. How to do business as a Christian ministry? We haven't done a lot in promoting business as ministry, perhaps because we had little systematic education in this area.

Education of business as ministry was an opportunity.

YouTube as Ministry

The Paul family had a YouTube channel whereby they documented their activities on their farm, including a wide range of agricultural practices such as planting, harvesting, gardening, milking, and even homeschooling. These activities were consistently showcased throughout the year, providing viewers insights into the family's agricultural endeavors and Christian ministries. As a direct observation by watching the Paul Family YouTube channel over a year, I noticed that a recurring caption that consistently appeared on the screen throughout each episode stated, "Everything we do is for the glory of the Lord." In connection to a question what he actually did to glorify God, Paul related his experiences and perspectives:

> To honor God, I'm not only preaching at the church. More importantly, I'm taking care of my family. I have seven children. I farm together with my dad. We have a YouTube channel, not for money but to share who we are and what we do on the farm and at the church. People know me not only as a farmer but also as a church pastor. People in need come to me 24/7. One day, a guy in the army called me at two o'clock in the morning, and he was having issues watching his baby. He said his baby was driving him nuts, and he was on the brink of shaking the baby; he was about ready to kill his own daughter, and he hated the thought of that. He's losing patience and knows he must call someone for help. He searched on the church's website and got my phone number. That's really a spiritual battle for me.
>
> Yes, I'm a church pastor, but I don't take income from the church. If pastoring is my spiritual gift from God, I don't think I should profit from my spiritual gift. That's my ministry. That's not a monetary thing. If there were any treasures out of it, I could have them in heaven. Apostle Paul was a tentmaker and a role model for us to follow.
>
> A local missionary in India watched our YouTube channel, and we got to know each other. After we had built up trust with each other,

we started to support him financially as our overseas missionary. I know our impact is small, but I live with a Christian example for my children and those watching our YouTube channel.

I farm for God's glory, I raise my family well for God's glory, I minister for God's glory, I run a YouTube channel for God's glory, and I steward my farmland for God. God is everything of my life, and everything we do is for the glory of God.

With his passion for the common good, Paul practiced his farming as ministry to glorify God. In other words, business as ministry for the common good manifested the glory of God.

If We Live Simply, Others Could Simply Live

A study participant with the pseudonym Anthony was a college student majoring in computer science. He spent the growing season (from spring to fall) as an intern at the

Catholic Worker Community Farm in 2023. He shared his experiences living on the farm:

> Living at the Catholic Worker Community Farm was just so very different from my normal life, far more rural. We don't have a toilet. We use a composting toilet, and the shower is much like a hose. It's like there's no AC [air conditioning]. But I feel like the people in the work ethic were really positive, and it was different from other jobs. I've done many things here. there's just so much love and positivity. There was not a lot of monetary reward, but lots of reward in other ways. I feel peaceful living and working here at the farm.
> During an interview with the founder of the Catholic Worker

Community Farm, Mary, it was revealed that she and her spouse had resided on the farm for over 15 years as of 2023. Mary proceeded to elucidate the concept of voluntary poverty, a doctrine rooted in Catholic Worker belief, which underpinned the organizational leadership:

> I made that choice myself. I want to live voluntarily in poverty because it gives me the ability to choose to do what I want with my time. And

this is what I want to do. It's because of its values. I believe that ethically and spiritually, in order for our planet to be okay, we all need to live a simple life. The rich people need to become poorer. Yeah, I don't think that anyone should live without enough food to eat or shelter to stay in, but we don't need excess. So, this is partly what I want to do in order to help the planet Earth a little bit. There should be more balance with the resources on the planet. But also partly, I think, it puts me in a place of more faith. Yes, instead of trusting my wealth and my power for my security and well-being, I want to trust my God. Yeah, choosing to live in voluntary poverty puts me in an exercise that makes me have more faith.

"Yes, if we live simply, others could simply live," I echoed. Those

who lived simply were passionate about the common good.

A Connection to the Land

Betty, a study participant, had an eating disorder and went to a clinic in

town. She was introduced to the Catholic Worker Community Farm to learn

about growing vegetables and eating. While weeding on the farm with Betty,

she said: "The philosophy of this farm is to bring hope to the poor.

"Do you consider yourself to be poor?" I asked.

"Yes, definitely," Betty said surely,

I'm a poor one. I'm poor with physical and emotional health. I believe that the community that is being formed here at the Catholic Worker Community Farm is quite important. How disconnected we are as a society. Our entire foodpurchasing procedure occurs behind closed doors, and we have no say in the matter. Just like with eating disorders, I believe it is critical to cultivate a connection to the land and to our food.

For me, just seeing the number of people who appreciate these resources and want to come out here and care about plants and the earth would be revolutionary because when you don't know everyone else, it can feel very lonely to be just carrying the issues over, and you can feel hopeless. Coming to the farm gives me a sense of making connections, both with people and nature.

Multiple informants, Mary, Christopher, Lisa, Jennifer, Patricia, George, Anthony, and Daniel described their connection to the land as a spiritual experience with intangible values.

A Safe Therapy

George, a study participant, was a commercial airline first officer pilot. During the 2023 growing season, he worked as a part-time farmworker at the Catholic Worker Community Farm. I was perplexed why he was willing to spend his very limited spare time at the farm during his incredibly hectic flight schedules. While we were weeding in the soil together, he explained,

> Well, I like flying. Flying isn't stressful at all, and it's actually quite enjoyable for me. It's all the other stuff, like dealing with maintenance difficulties or whether there are delays, that can be unpleasant. When I'm actually flying, you normally have a crew for a four-day trip, meet with them, and then you probably won't see them again. So, over the course of four days, you really get to know the crew, and although it's fun to meet new people, it can also be exhausting because you're always meeting someone new. I usually go home late from work, and then it's like going five legs a day sometimes, 12-hour work for days.
>
> I can see familiar faces while working as a part-time farmhand here. It's good to return to the farm and say, "Hey, Anthony, Mary, and Betty, what's up?" I just took a break and talked with my farm pals. Farming is a type of escape for me from the stresses of my job. Because we have to undergo a fresh medical check every 12 months, mental health is a very stigmatized aspect of flying. You cannot be on antidepressants and pass a medical examination. You cannot be taking antianxiety medicine, drinking alcohol, or using narcotics. Pilots are especially hesitant to seek organized counseling because they fear losing their medical license. And if they lose their medical, they will lose their job! So, farming is a kind of therapy, a safe therapy.

Betty, Lisa, Jennifer, and Christopher at the Catholic Worker Community Farm, as well as David and Barbara, among other study participants, also experienced their therapeutic journey while working on the farm or in their gardens. The study participants professed ministries like earthen vessels with Christ as their treasure inside to honor God.

In summary, the study participants experienced the significance of spiritual capital in the ministry and business contexts. They considered Christian values as the spiritual roots, culture as the spiritual soil, and ministry as a spiritual vessel, just as they regarded wisdom as the spiritual light that illuminated the way for both business and ministry ahead.

Social Capital—The Social Aspects

According to research participants' perspectives, what makes a business valuable is the good it does for the community. Through thematic coding, the primary components that formed the theme of social capital were relationships, trust, goodwill, and cooperation.

Relationships—The Social Assets

In accordance with the initial codes "an inner call," "transgenerational family heritage in farming," and "transgenerational family heritage in business," the

"relationships" category was established. Relationships were the social assets of a firm for both business and ministry to improve communication and collaboration and build strong networks and partnerships.

An Inner Call

> During an interview, Karen, a study participant, recounted her "inner call" story:

> I was a farm kid. I grew up with my parents and grandparents on a farm here in Iowa. At my age of eleven, my grandfather tragically took his own life. I did not much about it, and I did not know how to react

at that time. I did my undergrad here in Midwest, I just wanted to leave. I wanted to explore something new in the West Coast. So, I did my postgraduate Christian theological studies in California during the latter part of the 1980s. Like everyone in the seminary, I was expected to pursue a career as a clergy member in California following my completion of seminary. However, it was like there was an inner call deep in my heart, calling me to return home. Upon my arrival on our family farm in Northwestern Iowa in 1993, my grandparents' house had been entirely destroyed by a fire. There was an apple tree still alive. I transplanted the apple tree to my home garden so that I could be with him every day.

Karen felt fulfilled after discerning the meaning of the apple tree and reestablished her relationship with her grandfather.

Transgenerational Family Heritage in Farming

The study participant, identified as Thomas, was a research geneticist and university professor specializing in plant genetics. The individual spent most of his spare time in his community garden. In his undergraduate studies, Thomas took courses in mathematics and anthropology and continued his graduate studies in biology with research in plant genetics. He explained his transgenerational family heritage in this way:

Each child is a product of their genetics and environment, nature and nurture. In my case, my grandfather was a plant breeder and a gardener. My father was a mathematician, and my mother was an English professor. So, I acquired all of those. I loved being around my grandfather in his garden when I was small. I saw everything was beautiful.

Thomas perceived his relationship with his grandparents and parents as nature and nurture.

In his story, Brian, a study participant, disclosed:

I have been working as an accountant for the Iowa government since I graduated from college with an accounting degree. Five years ago, I retired in my mid-50s and have been working as a full-time farmer on our family farm. My grandfather was a dairy farmer in Illinois. My father, who grew up on a farm, pursued his studies until he obtained a Ph.D. degree in statistics. Subsequently, my father embarked on a career at the United States Department of Agriculture (USDA) in Washington, DC. However, my father eventually felt compelled to return to his agricultural roots. In the 1970s, my father secured employment at the National Animal Disease Laboratory (NADL) in Iowa. Concurrently, he engaged in farming on an 80-acre property nearby and retired from NADL at the age of 56.

When I was astonished by such a wonder in their lives, Brian described his father and him in this way, "We kind of use our passions for numbers in certainty to get better at farming with uncertainties." It seemed that the phenomenon of transgenerational family heritage pertained to both nature and nurture.

Transgenerational Family Heritage in Business

Joseph, another study participant, recounted his own narrative:

I'm a professor of computer science specializing in medical informatics at a university here in Iowa. Encouraged by the university entrepreneurship incubation program, I co-founded Joseph Medinformatics, a technology firm, alongside three other partners. Two of them are also professors and one is a medical doctor. The business, founded in 2009, had not been profitable yet as of 2023.

Regarding a question if his family has a business root, Joseph replied,

I don't think so. I just feel a bit difficult in those financial and legal aspects of the company. But we have the hearts to serve people. We have a passion to help doctors and patients. We'll keep working on it.

Business is an interdisciplinary study.

David, another study participant, shared his story:

I have been serving as a public-school administrator and educator for forty years. After we all retired, my wife, Barbara, and I looked for something to do. My grandfather was a college professor. He loved to grow things. He grew flowers like gladioli for fun. Additionally, he might have sold some of them as a side job. In my wife's family, Barbara's dad was a construction engineer. He worked as an engineer for a number of large companies and then started his own business to build and remodel buildings for many years. Barbara's mother had a kind of entrepreneurial background. Her grandfather started out as a kind of door-to-door salesman selling milking machines to farmers. And eventually, he built up his business to where he was a factory owner. Barbara often had ideas that we could start a business doing something. And so, when we got to the point of being retired, the cut flower business idea came out.

The phenomena of transgenerational familial legacy appeared to be related to

both nature and nurture.

When contemplating the reasons for the prominence of the cut flowers

business over other alternatives, one could not overlook the significance of

their transgenerational narratives:

David's grandfather was a college professor. He loved to grow things. He grew flowers like gladioli for fun. Additionally, he might have sold some of them as a side job. In Barbara's family, Barbara's dad was a construction engineer. He worked as an engineer for a number of large companies and then started his own business to build and remodel buildings for many years. Barbara's mother had a kind of entrepreneurial background. Her grandfather started out as a kind of doorto-door salesman selling milking machines to farmers. And eventually, he built up his business to where he was a factory owner. Barbara often had ideas that we could start a business doing something. And so, when we got to the point of being retired, the cut flower business idea came out.

Within the sample of 14 participants comprising business or farm

owners in this study, the owners of Donald Kevin Jason Family Farm,

William Conservation Farm,

Thomas Community Farm, David & Barbara Flower Farm, Karen Family Farm, Paul

Family Farm, Brian Family Farm, Robert & Sarah Farm, Elizabeth Tailor,

James Real Estate, exhibited a familial lineage characterized by a

transgenerational family heritage of faith, farming, or business. The degree to which organizational leaders aligned with their family heritage directly impacted the sustainability of their corporate operations and ministry endeavors.

The study participants believed that relationships provide stability and nourishment to social capital. Relationships are what anchor social networks and guide their actions just as roots provide stability and nourishment to a plant.

Trust—The Foundation of Social Capital

Following the emerging codes of "servanthood," "forgiveness and reconciliation," and "openness and appreciation build trust," the category of "trust" was established. Trust served as the foundation of social capital for business as ministry to thrive sustainably.

Servanthood

Emma, a client of the Deborah Salon, described her relationship with her cosmetologist, Deborah, in an interview:

> Once we got along as friends through a business relationship at her salon, Deborah would like to share her stories about how she connected with people in the community, particularly those newcomers from Asia, and introduced them to the church. Deborah had operated her hair salon business in town for over four decades. The Deborah Salon had become a literal community center for the Asian population. She always encouraged her clients to forgive each other for negative perceptions, repair a broken relationship, and help people resolve conflict peacefully and productively. She cared for both people's hair and souls.

Timothy, another customer of Deborah Salon, agreed with Emma that Deborah practiced servanthood through caring for people's tousles and souls. In an interview, Timothy shared his experience at the Deborah Salon:

> Initially, I felt that the business was just like a typical barbershop, providing haircut services to customers. But as time and conversations went by, I started feeling some characters and behaviors that might be associated with some kind of faith. At the time when she introduced me to a local Christian community church, I realized that Deborah was a Christian. She cared for me more than my hair. She always wanted to let me know how good the church is and how good the fellowship and the people are with similar backgrounds in language, culture, education, and ethnicity. A typical non-faith-based business would always be focusing on product and service promotion. They always wanted you to buy more and more; they always wanted to sell you something.

Timothy perceived servanthood as a good practice of the Deborah Salon to serve others more than its financial capital. Deborah's interest was beyond financial return.

Forgiveness and Reconciliation

From my field notes, the Catholic Worker Community Farm was registered as a farm instead of a tax-exempt non-profit. The farm was associated with the Catholic Worker Movement. The farm produced food for the community's poor and hungry. A substantial portion of the farm's produce was donated to local food pantries and soup kitchens. The farm also offered community education programs on sustainable agriculture and food justice. The farm demonstrated its core value of forgiveness and reconciliation by serving the impoverished and marginalized in the surrounding area and beyond.

As a farm worker at the Catholic Worker Community Farm, Jennifer shared her experience at the farm:

> I am a junior in college. I worked at the farm for about six hours a week during this growing season. Every week, I worked on the farm for three hours a day, from 7:00 am to 10:00 am, for two days. I paired

up with another trusted worker to practice forgiving ourselves and others and restoring our broken relationships with others and nature to make peace and build a healthy community. It's always
difficult to let our ego and pride go. It's a tough spiritual battle, I believe. I always had good conversations with my coworkers because we worked outside under sunlight and surrounded by nature. We discovered that working together in the sun, telling and listening to stories, was incredibly calming and healing.

The Catholic Worker Community Farm exemplified that Christian values such as forgiveness and reconciliation were differential and concrete elements of business as ministry for the common good. These elements were the foundation for building trust among the business stakeholders.

David and Barbara agreed that forgiveness and reconciliation were challenging spiritual battles. During an interview at their farm, David disclosed the symbolic meaning of the gate he built at the entrance of their flower garden:

> I have always felt a spiritual connection to working outdoors. Our garden has always been a place of peace for me, a place of my spiritual experience. When I worked under high stress with lots of challenging situations, including restoring broken relationships, going to and working in the garden was always peaceful, for the garden was a place of comfort and rest for me. So, I built that gate for entering the grounds of a spiritual setting. It's supposed to be passing into a place of peace. So, that was what I was thinking when I built that gate there.

David extended his spiritual battles to his garden and practiced forgiveness and reconciliation by restoring his relationships with God and nature. The gate served as a reminder to him that forgiveness and reconciliation were indeed spiritual encounters.

Openness and Appreciation Build Trust

When asked about how a horse farm established trust with its employees and customers, Robert and Sarah shared their practices and perspectives:

> The safety and well-being of our farm's workers and horses came first. We set up strict safety rules, gave everyone a lot of training, and created an environment that values feedback and open conversation. Safety is important to our business, which makes workers and customers feel safe and trusting. In all of our interactions with workers and customers, we were open and honest. We were honest about how we ran our horse farm, responded quickly to complaints, and kept our promises. This openness has built trust and made the farm's image as a trustworthy and honest business stronger. Our workers were important to us, so we treated them with respect and thanks. We gave farmworkers chances to learn how to ride horses for career growth and recognized their accomplishments. We even gave one of the farmhands a horse as a long service award. This positive experience for employees made them more loyal and involved, which in turn made customers happier.

The effort of Robert & Sarah Horse Farm to create trust has resulted in a devoted and supportive community of employees and consumers. The farm's dedication to safety, transparency, respect, and gratitude has made it a well-known and admired institution in the community. Informants Elizabeth, Deborah, Timothy, and Joseph concurred with Robert and Sarah that trust is established through openness and appreciation, based on their individual experiences.

The study participants perceived trust as a building's foundation. It kept social networks going and allowed them to develop.

Goodwill—The Currency of Social Capital

Goodwill was the currency of social capital, i.e., a builder of reputation and a bond with stakeholders. From the initial codes "hardworking," "willing to make the sacrifices necessary to help others," and "selflessness creates goodwill," the category of "goodwill" emerged.

Hardworking

"What do you think about the leadership of the farm?" I asked Anthony, an intern who lived at the Catholic Worker Community Farm. He responded,

> The farm leaders were working very hard. There wasn't much farm equipment, not even a horse. Human labor was used to complete almost everything. The leaders saw themselves as servants rather than leaders. Hardworking is a way of life for farm leaders. Their actions clearly speak louder than their words.

Mary, the farm's founder and leader had lived on the farm with her spouse for 15 years. She stated,

> I believe the Catholic Worker communities are generally a kind of voluntary poverty. I've been living and working here full-time for the past 15 years. I made that decision because I wish to live deliberately in poverty for its ethical and spiritual merits. I feel that for our earth to be okay, all of the rich people must become poorer.

Mary's life exemplified the reputation of the Catholic Worker Community Farm.

Willing to Make the Sacrifices Necessary to Help Others

> Christopher, another study participant, a farm worker at the Catholic Worker

Community Farm and an international student from India, stated,

> During the growing season [in 2023], I worked three hours per week as a parttime farmworker at the Catholic Worker Community Farm. Each

week, I received a box of fresh farm vegetables as compensation. The majority of the farm's fresh produce was delivered to local food pantries to help the poor and disenfranchised. The farm leaders were not only working hard but also living hard. For 15 years, they chose to live in voluntary simplicity and voluntary poverty. They didn't even have adequate medical coverage or a modern toilet. It's difficult for me to believe that this is a reality in 21st-century American society. In my perspective, it is completely unnecessary. However, they chose their way of life. They are willing to make the necessary sacrifices to help others.

By making the sacrifices required to aid others, the leaders of the Catholic Worker

Community Farm exhibited voluntary simplicity and voluntary poverty.

Selflessness Creates Goodwill

Karen, a research participant, donated 60 acres of her farmland to the Iowa Natural Heritage Foundation in 2011 while continuing to practice organic farming on the remainder of her farmland. Karen distributed free tomato seedlings to the community and sponsored plant and pizza events where people could learn about gardening and enjoy a free lunch. She also gave the neighborhood free pullet chicks. Karen received the Farmland Owner Award from Practical Farmers of Iowa in 2013 in recognition of her efforts to preserve and improve her farm.

Karen's selflessness has built Karen Family Farm a goodwill that contributed to the social capital of her endeavor. James, Deborah, Joseph, Sarah, Paul, Donna, Joshua, David, Barbara, Linda, William, and Mary, among other business owners, concurred with Karen that a business goodwill could be established by selflessness.

The study participants' "hardworking," "sacrifices," and "selflessness" were categorized into goodwill as the currency of social capital, just as money is a country's currency. Goodwill enabled informants to share ideas, resources, and opportunities.

Cooperation—The Social Cohesion

"Cooperation" as a category arose from the initial codes of "everyone is seen as equal," "consensus enhanced cooperation," and "a supportive and collaborative work environment." in the context of business as ministry, cooperation served as the social cohesion of social capital for aligning with Christian values and building a strong faithbased organization for its sustainability.

Everyone Is Seen as Equal

Jennifer, a study participant, was a neuroscience major student in college. She participated in the work-for-food program at the Catholic Worker Community Farm for three growing seasons. Jennifer loved the communal work and offered her opinions and experiences at the farm:

> I kind of liked the work environment out here while harvesting and weeding with people at the farm. It felt like it was free of inferiority, facework, comparison, competition, self-interest, hierarchy, social prestige, and financial hardship. When it comes to the farm, we don't need any social or financial standing or influence; we're all just farm workers. Everyone is seen as equal.

Jennifer believed equality encouraged cooperation.

Consensus Enhanced Cooperation

In a conversation about the leadership style at the Catholic Worker Community

Farm, Mary, the founder and the leader of the farm, explained:

We use a consensus system to make decisions. This system is based on the

Catholic Worker's concept of Personalism, the Catholic Personalism, or say, Christian Personalism. We emphasize the dignity of each individual. So, a consensus system will enable more considered, inclusive, and cooperative decision-making. The farm leadership team meet once on a Sunday afternoon per month to discuss and make decisions about all issues of the farm, including planting, harvesting, marketing, and financing. These meetings are open to all participants. All the farm leadership team members are required to attend regularly. To make a decision, we encourage brainstorming, discussion, and sometimes we vote for issues. If the team could not reach an agreement on a specific issue, we could postpone the issues until a later meeting. Frankly speaking, we need patience for good decisions to be made.

A Supportive and Collaborative Work Environment

Throughout two promotional events held at the William Conservation Farm for the local farmers, William described how his farm improved its community and farmworker collaboration. Six ideas were distilled from my field notes: The first was pursuing a common goal of conservation of water and soil of the farmland with its farmworkers and rural community members. The second was creating a supportive and collaborative work environment in the farm. The third was giving farmworkers a voice in decision-making and supporting the research and development of water and soil conservation technology experiments and implementation on the farm. The fourth was sourcing supplies or services that were ethical, sustainable, and socially responsible for the water and soil conservation projects of the farm. The fifth was partnering with other businesses, non-profit organizations, and local government agencies to share resources, expertise, and knowledge for the common goal. Finally, the sixth was working with the community to address social and environmental issues with its resources and competencies in the expertise of farmland water and soil conservation.

Cooperation was a valuable asset for the William Concertation Farm to foster its social value on the market and its ministry in the community.

In summary, the study participants described the value of social capital in the ministry and business contexts. They implied trust as the foundation of social capital, goodwill as the currency of social capital, and cooperation as social cohesion, just as they regarded relationships as the social assets that anchored social networks and supported their business and ministry.

Intellectual Capital—The Intellectual Aspects

The intangible asset of a firm is what makes it valuable inherently. The theme of intellectual capital was formulated from the thematic coding of the following four primary categories: creativity, insight, brand, and systems.

Creativity—An Intellectual Catalyst

In this study, the "creativity" category was created by using focus coding on the following codes: "everyone is valued for their unique gifts and talents," "watch what we do to know what we believe," and "children's creativity could be nurtured." Creativity had a distinct and dynamic role in the intellectual capital of business as ministry. It served as a catalyst for both internal and external growth, forging deeper connections and increasing the ministry's influence in the community.

Everyone Is Valued for Their Unique Gifts and Talents

Another farmworker, Lisa, described her experiences at the Catholic Worker

Community Farm:

> At the farm, we respect each other as farm workers. Some people have a gift of communication; some have a gift of green thumb; some have a rose, others have a thorn, and some have a bud. I valued my hands when I saw my hands in the soil helping the plants develop; when I harvested the vegetables and carried them to those in need, I valued my hands. The work we've done on the farm has benefited not only ourselves but also others in the community, particularly those in need. As a result of our labor at the farm, everyone is valued for their unique gifts and talents.

These unique gifts and talents were the abilities to generate new ideas and solutions that align with the farm's mission and values.

Watch What We Do to Know What We Believe

"If you want to know what we believe, watch what we do," David replied when I questioned if their cut flower business is based on a belief doctrine. The reply was exactly how the David & Barbara Flower Farm operated.

David believed creativity could be fostered. Mary, Thomas, William, Linda, and Barbara were all in accord with David's faith when he said, "If you want to know what we believe, watch what we do."

Children's Creativity Could Be Nurtured

Paul, a study participant, believed creativity was both nature and nurture. In addition to the conventional children's activities at the farm, He fostered his children's creativity by delegating the production and management of the Paul Family Farm YouTube channel to his children. Children took charge of the video taking, editing, and publishing freely. Their professional-level drone footage and editing with soundtracks demonstrated their creativity beyond their age. As Paul stated:

Kids were brought to the theme park of creativity. They had a lot of fun doing YouTube. You could see their tireless smiling faces on our YouTube channel all year. We were able to reach missionaries in India and people in need in Africa through this YouTube channel. God really uses our tube as His vessel for us to integrate our farming with our Christian faith as a ministry for His glory. Paul's Christian values and culture in his family fostered his children's holistic thrive, much like the rich black soil on his farm cultivated crops to grow healthily.

The study participants implied that creativity played a distinct and dynamic function in the social capital of business as ministry. It served as a catalyst for both internal and external growth, fostering deeper connections and strengthening the ministry's impact within the community.

Insight—A Deep Understanding

The "insight" category was formed in this study by the utilization of focus coding on the codes "a life-long learning," "passion for farming," and "passion for business."
Insight was crucial in managing the organization's particular challenges and opportunities. It went beyond mere knowledge or information. It was a deep understanding of building a link between data and wisdom, directing the business and ministry toward effective mission fulfillment and sustainable growth.

A Life-Long Learning

William was a professor at a university in Minnesota and the farm owner of the William Conservation Farm, which is located in Iowa. William laid out the vision and mission of the farmland conservation for Daniel, the farmer who rented the farm from the William family, to carry out. William offered his beliefs and experiences when I asked him how to preserve a sustainable relationship between the farm owner and the farmer toward a conservation goal:

> For a long-term sustainable relationship with the farmers, farm owners should set our self-interest aside for the sake of preserving our farmlands for future generations. We should appreciate and treat our farmers fairly and honestly by absorbing the increased costs of water and soil conservation in comparison to conventional farming practices. In my scenario, I assumed the additional costs of introducing cover crops, building two saturated buffers and one bioreactor, and constructing multiple terraces. I oversee public relations with government agencies, non-profit conservation organizations, and university research institutes. I'm also responsible for promoting our conservation methods to other local farm owners and farmers. To do all of this, you must be passionate about stewardship of our land and the planet; to be passionate about stewardship, you must have some beliefs and values.

As a farm owner, William used his insight to motivate his farmer to work on creation care constantly. Mary, Donald, Kevin, and Paul, among other business as ministry leaders, used their insights to establish role models for the farm workers to follow.

Passion for Farming

During the planting season of 2023, I had the privilege of piloting the John Deere planter with Kevin, a participant in this study. We had a productive conversation for three hours, and I thoroughly relished my time farming in the Midwest. In the second interview with Kevin, I thanked him for the opportunity to gain experiential knowledge from him and inquired, "How many acres did you plant that day?"

"About 400 acres," he responded.
"Wow! More than that of the whole farm of many other single-family farms," I was startled and intrigued by the answer. "How many hours did you spend planting those 400 acres?"

"I worked from eight in the morning until ten at night."

"Fourteen hours! You worked very hard, Kevin." I was astounded by the rural Midwestern culture and continued my inquiry: "I understand that you and I enjoyed our three-hour conversation in the morning, but what about the other eleven hours? Were you bored sitting alone inside the tractor?"

He chuckled and continued with his enthusiasm:

> I didn't feel bored at all. I was mostly just thinking of the plants growing. Looking at the three monitors in the John Deere tractor, I was always thinking about planting these acres and the next acres, this field, and the next field. I don't have a radio or entertainment with me. I Just watching the GPS monitors and thinking of having a good harvest this year. I'm always thinking about how great the harvest is going to be. And if it's a bad harvest, I'm thinking how great the next year is going to be. We're always optimistic about what is coming. Sometimes, I was looking at neighbors' farms and thinking of renting or buying their farms, thinking about the expansion of our farm. I was always excited about it. There's always hope, a hope on seeds breaking through the soil, clouds breaking into the rain, and plants growing stronger and larger, just like many Bible analogies and references in agriculture. As farmers, we always have a positive attitude to overcome negative attitudes, anxiety, or depression. I just always loved farming.

Farming is also a part of the life of a farmer with a passion for the common good.

Passion for Business

Elizabeth Tailor's fashion business was positioned at the reuse and repurposing of clothing. During an interview on a topic about her passion to start up such a niche business, Elizabeth, the owner of the business, expressed:

> My mother was a dietician. My father is a pastor. Their parents were farmers. I studied fashion design at college. In our family, we are concerned with a sustainable ecosystem more than consumerism, more than the American culture of "bigger, better, newer, the best." You don't need to be rich to have a comfortable life.

> "Yes, if we live simply on the earth, the planet earth could simply live," I resonated.

Passionate Christian business leaders were driven by their faith to use their businesses to promote the common good. Study participants saw their businesses as more than just a way to make money; they deeply understood their businesses as a platform for positively impacting the world.

Brand—The Personality of Business

In the framework of business as ministry, a brand serves as the firm's personality, based on concepts such as humanizing the business, authenticity, consistency, emotional connection, and uniqueness. In this study, the "brand" category was established through the implementation of focus coding on the following codes: "soil is beautiful and powerful," "slow as a brand," and "growing brand value through community services."

Soil Is Beautiful and Powerful

Betty, a study participant, suffered from an eating disorder and sought treatment at a local clinic. She was brought to the Catholic Worker

Community Farm to learn about gardening and eating. Betty told her account

about the farm's impact on her life:

> I was patiently waiting for the growing season to resume during the months when I was in school. I enjoy going to school. I enjoy studying, but I also enjoy getting my hands dirty in the soil. I'm still learning. This summer, I learned a lot about sustainability, seasonal produce, and growing food for a community, and I also got the opportunity to organize community events at the farm.
>
> I can sense the aliveness of this place. Just swimming around with the soil in your hands, with all the birds tipping, all the bees, butterflies, and everything. It's almost as if there's energy, you can sense how alive everything is, especially when working on the garlic beneath the soil, which was black. The soil was beautiful and powerful, and everything felt so joyful. It just feels like the earth is glad to return the favor. You can breathe a little bit more out here. "People usually use the word 'dirt' to describe soil. Why did you use 'beauty' and

'power' instead?" I was intrigued by the language she used.

Betty continued excitedly:

Because soil is absolutely everything, it is always filling this entire farm, and everything goes into it. There are so many living organisms in the soil on my hands. Microorganisms exist. It is a vital source of life. It all begins there. Everything begins with those soil ties. It's called the life cycle. It truly is. So, soil is a part of life.

"Yeah, life is beautiful; life is powerful," I reinforced.

Betty couldn't stop:

It changed my whole perspective on food, eating, gratitude, and respect for all the things that go into it because it's not as simple as ordering a plate with meatballs. I developed a connection with the people on the farm; I learned that soil must be conserved and cared for since it is vital to the entire ecosystem, and I feel a connection to the food I eat. That enabled me to be healthy in so many ways.

A strong brand reputation helped Catholic Worker Community Farm

attract and retain interns, farm workers, customers, and community partners with positive word-ofmouth promotions. Several study participants, namely Anthony, George, Lisa, Christopher, and Patricia, all concurred with Betty's experience that "soil is beautiful and powerful."

Slow as a Brand

Elizabeth Tailor positioned its high-quality clothing and tailoring services in a slow fashion. This brand strategy was based on her Christian values of stewardship of the community members and planet Earth. Elizabeth said, "You don't need to be rich to have a comfortable life." The brand consistently received a rating of 4.7 (out of 5.0) stars on social media reviews. Elizabeth Tailor was a well-respected brand with a strong reputation in

Iowa. The business's high brand value resulted from its commitment to quality, customer service, and community involvement. Indeed, you don't need to spend a lot of money to have a comfortable brand.

"You do not require much financial capital to establish a meaningful YouTube brand," Paul, the proprietor of Paul Family Farm, concurred with Elizabeth.

Growing Brand Value Through Community Services

During a conservation promotion event at his farm for the farmers in Iowa,

William, a study participant, shared his experiences in partnering with local communities:

> We value our involvement and partnership with the local community. We organize educational events such as field trips, workshops, and school visits. At these events, people could learn about our farm history and sustainable agriculture. We maintain good relationships

with several neighborhood groups, including local organizations involved in soil and water conservation, natural heritage, and the community school district.

William Conservation Farm established a strong brand through community involvement. John, Donna, Elizabeth, and Joshua were among the informants who mentioned that community services may help build a strong brand for the company.

The research participants designed their brands to be like the personality of their organizations, generating economic value while also contributing substantially to intellectual capital through authenticity, consistency, emotional connection, and originality. A brand is what makes a business unique and memorable. It might be friendly, sustainable, professional, cultural, amusing, or solemn.

Systems—The Infrastructure of Intellectual Capital

In the context of business as ministry, systems were the principles, frameworks, and processes that kept the business and the ministry working smoothly and efficiently. The present study utilized focus coding to establish the "systems" category, which comprised of the following codes: "family-owned and operated agriculture system," "personnel system," "crop production system," "livestock system," "gardening system," "business system," "ministry system," "financial system," "social media system," "homeschooling system,"

"community-supported agriculture system" and "water and soil conservation systems."

Family-Owned and Operated Agriculture System

According to my field notes, family-owned and operated agriculture refers to a mode of agricultural production characterized by individual families' ownership and operation of farms. The prevailing form of agriculture in the United States was family farms, which constituted more than 90% of the total farms. The Paul Family Farm was owned and operated by Paul, his parents, his spouse, and their three children, who comprised a singular family unit. Additionally, they own three swine houses, each containing 1,200 hogs. Paul shared his knowledge about family-owned and operated agriculture with experience of his farm as an example:

> In our case, some of my ancestors came to America from Scotland actually on Mayflower. Some came over on the same boat as William Penn, which was shortly after the Mayflower. Most of my ancestry in America was in North Carolina. They had been there for two hundred fifty years or so, then we moved out here in Iowa. We moved out here because the big city kept getting bigger and bigger and bigger. And they did not like farmers. They wanted my dad's farm for housing development, and my dad knew that Iowa was an agricultural area. So, we came out here, and it's been nice for 30 years. Today, my parents, my wife and I own and operate the farm together with my children.

Paul introduced several organizational systems within his farm, such as people, crop production, livestock, gardening, small business, ministry, financial, social media, and homeschooling systems.

Personnel System

Paul managed his farm's personnel system by organizing the human resources into two teams:

> My dad and I, together with my three children, work as a farming team. My wife is leading the housekeeping team with the rest of the

family members. We may hire two to three additional agricultural laborers during the hectic planting and harvesting seasons.

Crop Production System

Crop production in the Midwestern United States was a professional and industrial endeavor. Paul explained what it meant:

> Crop production includes all agricultural aspects from planting and irrigation to fertilizing and harvesting. Our farming team handle the crop production with two tractors, one combine, one planter, a sprayer, a fertilizer spreader, a hay baler, a mower, a loader, a forklift, a grain dryer, a grain cart, and two large grain bins.

Livestock System

Paul outsourced the livestock system to external professionals: "Others outside of the family operated the hog business commercially. The family keep hens, sheep, milk cows, horses, and a mule for self-sufficiency and education purposes. The family's farming team manages the livestock system daily."

Gardening System

Paul's wife led the housekeeping team to manage the garden. Paul said: "A garden on the farm usually produces enough vegetables for the family all year. The housekeeping team manages the garden. The team is also in charge of all household chores at home."

Business System

Paul also ran a small business online. He introduced the business: "We own the intellectual property for the farm's trademark and run an online store selling farm-themed merchandise such as T-shirts, caps, Carhartt hoodies, and crochet plush animals. Our children run this small online business."

Ministry System

In addition to being a farmer, Paul was also a church pastor responsible

for local community church ministry and overseas missions. Paul shared:

> We planted a church in a neighboring community in 2012. I've been
> serving as a pastor at the church without receiving financial pay from
> the church since then. The church serves the community with a
> population of 25,000 people. Through our YouTube channel, we also
> proclaim the gospel and encourage doing farming and business
> together with Christian values. We have also been financially
> supporting a local missionary in India, who contacted us through our
> YouTube channel. We've been very blessed in all the ministries we've
> done for the glory of God.

Financial System

Paul was involved in financial systems of the farm, the church, and the

overseas missions. He explained the systemic operation:

> We separate the church's financial system from our farm's and keep
> the tithe and offering at the church in our personal domain. The tithe
> and offering budget at the church as well as for the financial support to
> overseas missions was steady year after year, with no particular
> connection to our agricultural or business income.

Social Media System

Social media was regarded as a modern vessel of evangelism. Paul

described his experiences with this contemporary instrument:

> In February 2010, we launched a YouTube channel. The children were
> in charge of video taking, editing, and publishing for the channel. They
> had a lot of fun particularly with their beloved drone's eyes. We've
> produced over 440 videos; we have over 240 thousand subscribers;
> and we have received over 110 million views on the channel. On every
> episode, we posted the same message: "Everything we do is for the
> Glory of the Lord."

Homeschooling System

Homeschooling was ideal for the agricultural seasons in the Midwest
of the United

States. Paul elaborated:

> On the farm, all of my children were homeschooled so that they could work more during planting, usually in May and harvesting seasons in November, and study more in the off seasons. We have different systems and seasons than those in schools.

Community-Supported Agriculture System

Christopher, a study participant, was familiar with community-supported agriculture. He recounted his knowledge and experience during an interview:

> I'm a college student. I was working on a community project locally in town to explore community supported agriculture. So, I joined the Catholic Worker Community Farm. Community Supported Agriculture (CSA) is an agricultural system that facilitates the connection between consumers and farmers within a local community, like farm-to-table. The Catholic Worker Community Farm is a typical CSA. CSA members provide financial or labor support to local farmers in exchange for a share of the farm's fresh, seasonal produce on a weekly basis, spanning the duration of the cultivation period. CSA contributes to the connection of people and the connection with nature.

Water and Soil Conservation Systems

The systems established and executed by William, Daniel, and Linda at the William Conservation Farm contained a number of beneficial water and soil conservation initiatives. From my field notes, these initiatives as parts of the water and soil conservation system included:

Coverage cropping: In the off-season, cover crops were sown to protect the soil from erosion and fertilizer runoff. The William Conservation Farm grew cover crops such as rye, oats, and radishes.

No-till agriculture: No-till farming is a technique that reduces soil disturbance. This improves soil health and reduces erosion.

Saturated buffers: Saturated buffers were areas of grassland or wetland flooded by water. This aided in filtering nutrients and sediment from runoff before it enters streams and rivers.

Woodchip bioreactors: Woodchip bioreactors were trenches filled with woodchips that aided in removing nitrate from tile water. Water that had drained through the soil and into a network of underground pipes was referred to as tile water.

In addition, the William Conservation Farm collaborated with various organizations to promote and execute conservation techniques. The farm, for example, collaborated with the local County Soil and Water Conservation District to provide field days and workshops for other farmers and landowners.

The conservation efforts at William Conservation Farm substantially impacted water quality in the Four Mile Creek watershed. For example, Iowa State University Extension research discovered that the farm's saturated buffers reduced nitrate levels in tile water by up to 90%.

The William Conservation Farm was a sustainable agriculture approach. The farm's conservation dedication showed the feasibility of producing food while safeguarding the environment. The study participants, Paul, Mary, Christopher, William, Kevin, and Elizabeth considered corporate systems as the infrastructure of their enterprises, which were responsible for the growth and development of intellectual capital.

In brief, the study participants were exposed to the significance of intellectual capital in both business and ministry settings. The informants conceptualized insight as a deep understanding, corporate systems as an infrastructure of intellectual capital, akin to how they perceived creativity as an intellectual spark that ignited a fire of intellectual capital and empowered the organization for innovation and development.

Summary of the Findings

According to the findings, research participants believed that a profitable business as a Christian ministry has its own financial, spiritual, social, and intellectual capital to glorify God. The business as ministry stakeholders in the rural Midwestern United States experienced and perceived that profit, cash, debt, and assets are all examples of financial capital, constituting the financial aspects of their business as ministry for the common good. They also experienced and perceived that wisdom, values, culture, and ministry are all components of spiritual capital that represent the spiritual aspects of the common good in their business as ministry. They also experienced and perceived that relationships, trust, goodwill, and cooperation all contribute to social capital, which can be categorized as the social aspects of the common good in their business as ministry. They also experienced and perceived that intellectual capital encompasses creativity, insight, brand, and systems. The subsequent chapters will discuss the interconnection and interactions of financial, spiritual, social, and intellectual capital for the common good.

Chapter 6

Discussion

This basic qualitative study aimed to understand how the business as ministry stakeholders in the rural Midwestern United States practiced and perceived business as ministry for the common good. The primary understanding that emerged from this study was that business as ministry stakeholders in rural Midwestern US believed that business as ministry has its own financial, spiritual, social, and intellectual capital for the common good. Financial capital includes profit, cash, debt, and assets. Wisdom, values, culture, and ministry sustain spiritual capital. Relationships, trust, goodwill, and cooperation influence social capital. Creativity, insight, brand, and systems are all examples of intellectual capital. The financial, spiritual, and social capital correspond with the research questions and the published literature on the subject. This chapter explores the interconnection and interactions of these capitals for the common good.

Financial Capital

Financial capital refers to the monetary resources available to a business in order for it to operate and grow. It is the lifeblood of any business, allowing it to buy necessary assets, cover expenses, and invest in future business opportunities (Brealey et al., 2020). In this study, the research participants experienced and perceived the financial capital of a profit-making business as a Christian ministry as its aggregate value of the financial resources, including profit, cash, debt, and assets. These resources were able to potentially allocate funds toward the organization's operational activities, facilitate investments in novel avenues for expansion, and provide sustenance to its Christian ministry.

Profit

According to study participants, profit is the lifeblood of their enterprises, but not life itself. An adequate blood supply is required for life to survive, but the purpose of life is not to produce blood. Nevertheless, maximizing blood production is not a sufficient condition for life to thrive. Blood is a means to a life; profit is a means to the common good (Van Duzer, 2010). Blood production should not harm other body organs; thus, business as ministry should be profitable but not exploitative. Business as ministry has a long-term goal, as long as future generations can profit. Short-term considerations are either for survival or speculation, which could negatively affect others and the earth's ecosystems.

Cash

Cash is the physical currency and bank deposits that a company has on hand. Generally, cash is produced through investments, sales of products or services, and customer collections, among other things. Cash flow, on the other hand, is the movement of money into and out of business over time. It measures how much cash a company makes or spends in a certain period. Cash flow is vital to sustainability because it enables companies to fulfill their financial obligations, invest in expansion, and return capital to shareholders. Generally, a company with robust cash flow is regarded as being in sound financial condition.

According to the findings, farming is considered a low-cash and high-asset business. Farmers' cash-flow management is crucial to their financial stability because their enterprises frequently run on thin margins and face seasonal swings in revenue and expenditures. Farmers practiced the law of gratitude in addition to the typical financial strategies. They did not consider their ministry giving as an expense in the cash-flow formula but as an investment in reflecting God's glory and light to those in need by offering their financial resources. What was in their recipe were God's blessings on their lives and farms throughout the course of years and generations. Other study participants placed their personal health and business peace into the formula. The formula is a method of long-term cash-flow management in business as ministry for the common good. It is a cash-flow management culture built on faith. In the work-for-food program of the Catholic Worker Community Farm, although workers were paid by food, a traditional way of compensation for work involved no cash, and the participants' physical, psychological, and spiritual experiential values were beyond the monetary meanings of the work.

Debt

The findings indicate that debt has the potential to either leverage or destroy a business. It incorporates inherent risk-taking attributes of the business environment. Faith plays a pivotal role in navigating and overcoming uncertainties as well as saving lives. When investors supported a business as ministry with microloans with no interest, the returns on investment (ROIs) were not cash equivalents. The values of those microloans to the creditors might not be in financial terms. As C. N. Johnson (2009) described, these microloan programs are devoted to and support the development of the least-resourced communities. The individual and institutional investors shared the same values and vision of the business as ministry. Thus, they also practiced finance as ministry for the common good. The ROIs of the investments could then be in spiritual terms.

Assets

A business asset is an economically valuable resource under the ownership or control of a firm that is anticipated to yield future advantages. Assets may be intangible or tangible. Tangible assets are visible and touchable physical goods. Property, plant, equipment, inventories, and cash equivalents are examples of tangible assets. Intangible assets are non-physical goods with monetary value. Intangible assets encompass a variety of items, including intellectual property, goodwill, accounts receivable, and investments.

This study discovered that a business as ministry asset could be an economically, psychologically, or spiritually valuable resource under the ownership or control of a firm expected to provide future benefits among business as ministry stakeholders for the common good. The valuables in

Deborah's instance were health and peace; in Karen's case, her wishes came true; and in Joseph's situation, there were perceived assets.

Spiritual Capital

According to Zohar and Marshall (2011), spiritual capital is the worth and potential that spirituality and ethical values may provide to individuals and organizations. The notion of spiritual capital within a business as ministry organization refers to the collective value of intangible assets that are intrinsically linked to its Christian faith and its various ministries and missions. The assets in this context include the organization's mission and values, culture, and relationships with stakeholders (O'Sullivan & Flanagan, 2017; Cullen et al., 2010). In this study, the spiritual capital of business as ministry was found to be associated with Christian wisdom, values, culture, and ministry.

Wisdom

The current study revealed that wisdom, serving as a fundamental component of spiritual capital, played a decisive role in shaping business as ministry. William, a study participant, had a vision that extended to future generations. Spirituality and ethical principles were valued not for their monetary worth but for their relationship with God as stewards of His creation. Wisdom is, therefore, the capacity to assess the long-term repercussions of decisions and ensure that they serve the overall mission and goals of the firm.

The conversation with Richard, a study participant, was fascinating in the natural and social sciences intersection. Richard contributed knowledge to the discussion by recognizing the distinctions between intangible and tangible, instrumental and intrinsic, as well as certainty and uncertainty. Science and technology might offer a common good but can also bring a common evil. A common evil could thus suggest a lack of understanding in balancing a business's financial and spiritual capital for the common good.

The Catholic Worker Community Farm's leadership demonstrated their wisdom by making ethical decisions in all their transactions, learning from experience, and seeking assistance from others.

This study highlighted the significance of wisdom as a fundamental component of spiritual capital in business as ministry for the common good. Wisdom is not just an abstract concept but a practical tool that aids in making informed and ethical decisions, considering both immediate and long-term impacts. It transcends monetary valuation, emphasizing a deeper connection with ethical and spiritual principles rooted in stewardship of God's creation. By embodying wisdom, business as ministry can enrich its operations and foster a community where both the business and its stakeholders thrive together.

Values

The present study discovered that values, as an essential element of spiritual capital, exerted a pivotal influence on business as ministry. In the Donald Kevin Jason Family

Farm, the Christian values of faith, hope, and love were regarded as the guiding principles of family farming. James Real Estate was compassionate and understanding of the financial concerns of the single-mother family tenants. James prioritized empathy and kindness before rent. As a result, he had flexible payment schedules and even forgave rentals for those in need. According to his tenant, Edward, "James made a difference in the community through his Christian character of showing mercy to others." Joshua and Donna, two study participants, grew sweetcorn for the prisoners for free for several years. They felt that serving the people in need has a spiritual value in and of itself.

According to Ciulla (2020), the values of a business are the guiding principles that inform its decisions and actions. They are the "why" underlying a company's actions and should be consistent with its purpose and vision. Participants in this study created and increased their business values by providing high-quality products and services that meet the needs of their customers, being honest and ethical in all dealings, treating stakeholders respectfully and fairly, focusing on serving others, and being responsible stewards of their resources, and treating others with empathy and kindness. The Christian faith of the stakeholders, notably the organization's leaders, shaped business as ministry values.

Culture

This study found that culture, being an intrinsic component of spiritual capital, played a crucial role in business as ministry. For the Donald Kevin

Jason Family Farm, the organizational culture of a family legacy was defined by five generations. The core values of a missional family farm were shared by local and overseas missionaries all over the world. The farm's organizational culture was nourished by Christian faith.

Paul, a research participant, had responsibilities as both a farmer and a priest.

However, he firmly positioned himself as a farmer and did not take income from the role of church pastor. This precise positioning developed the Paul family farm's organizational culture of business as ministry rather than ministry as business.

Elizabeth Tailor created and maintained its organizational culture by positioning the company as slow fashion with excellence in products and services, hiring for cultural fit in slow culture, encouraging employee feedback, and recognizing behavior compatible with the firm's core values.

The slow food culture introduced by Professor Thomas was a mirror reflecting the nature of fast-food business culture in America. According to Thomas, if we can be slow enough, we will see that everyone is sacred, and everything is holy. When we see that everyone is sacred and everything is holy, there will be an ultimate equilibrium in humanity, where all available niches in all ecosystems will be filled with diversity in all lives. The culture will be the glory of God, the common good culture.

In this study, a healthy organizational culture cultivated healthier business stakeholders, resulting in higher business returns with high-quality products and services. A healthy organizational culture was also more resistant to egoism, individualism, materialism, consumerism, racism, and even active warfare both there and here (Felber, 2019). Furthermore, a healthy organizational culture contributes to the balance of demand and supply regarding products and services, innovation for the firm, and sustainability for planet Earth (Van Duzer, 2010). Participants in this study created and maintained an organizational culture by defining the culture with their core values and sharing their values, beliefs, and behaviors through congruent and reciprocal communication, led by example, hired and promoted for cultural fit, encouraged employee feedback, rewarded and recognized behavior, and continuously monitored and adjusted. The common good culture of business as ministry was perceived as the ultimate equilibrium in humanity in all aspects, the manifestation of God's glory (Hollenbach, 2017).

Ministry

As an instrumental part of spiritual capital, ministry played a practical role in business as ministry in this study. According to John, a pastor of a local community church, some niches of the systematic education of business as ministry still need to be filled out at the church level. This study illuminated the need for both scholarship development and practitioner education of business as ministry, which can be regarded as forms of education as ministry.

According to informant Paul, who encouraged his children to operate a YouTube channel to share their Christian farm life, the purpose of the

YouTube channel was not for profit-making business but as a Christian ministry to reach out to the people in need and witness God's glory through their life-to-life impacts to save lives. They reached out to the veterans desperate in need; they reached out to the local Indian missionary in financial need; and they reached out to many people around the world by preaching with life examples. This ministry's return on spiritual capital investment was much more significant than those financials for the family, the farm, and the church.

A ministry of the Catholic Worker Community Farm was to offer opportunities for people to live on the farm to experience voluntary simplicity and voluntary poverty to understand and resonate with the poor. Living in voluntary simplicity might not generate much wealth in monetary terms, but it would produce spiritual capital. Voluntary poverty might not make people rich in wealth. Still, it could keep people's conceptualization of serving people in need distinguished from "Giving your extra to the poor as a charity" or "Money does not grow on trees." As a result, those living on the farm became rich in spiritual capital.

As experienced by the study participants at the Catholic Worker Community Farm, the connection to people and nature was rich in spiritual capital. Those who were mentally poor were treated with a safe therapy of connection to people and nature on the farm.

Ministry is an essential component of spiritual capital in business as ministry, playing a practical role in fostering the common good. This study highlighted the need for systematic education and practitioner training of business as ministry, which can be regarded as forms of education as ministry. Living in voluntary simplicity might not generate much wealth in monetary terms, but it would produce spiritual capital. Voluntary poverty might not make people rich in wealth. Still, it could keep people's conceptualization of serving people in need distinguished from "Giving your extra to the poor as a charity" or "Money does not grow on trees." As a result, those living in voluntary simplicity and voluntary poverty became rich in spiritual capital.

The findings suggest that Christian ministry can generate and preserve spiritual capital through individual, community, and creation care for the common good. In summary, from the study participants' experiences and perceptions, spiritual capital is associated with wisdom in the use of knowledge and experience for the common good, Christian values as guiding principles that inform a company's decisions and actions, Christian culture that shapes how stakeholders interact, and ministry that the business carries out intrinsically and instrumentally for the common good.

Social Capital

According to McCann (2011), social capital is "the network of connections of trust, dependability, and rule-following, all of which are required for any type of civic coexistence" (p.56). According to Lovrich and Pierce (2016), organizational social capital pertains to the assortment of resources accessible to an organization by means of its social networks.

According to Sorenson and Milbrandt (2023), family social capital in the context of family business is the network of social connections marked by goodwill and trust that exists among families who own firms. According to the findings of this study, business as ministry social capital was found to be associated with relationships among stakeholders, including the community, trust between the company and its stakeholders, goodwill that contributes to the company's reputation and market value, and cooperation between parties to pursue the common good.

Relationships

Relationships, being a crucial component of social capital, exerted a significant impact on the implementation of business as ministry in this study. Karen's grandfather was a stakeholder in Karen Family Farm. Karen's relationship with her grandfather was a source of social capital that propelled her from the Midwest to California and from the cosmopolitan Bay Area of California to her agricultural roots in Iowa, USA. That social capital encouraged Karen to donate 60 acres of farmland to the Iowa Natural Heritage Foundation. Social capital is valuable in all its forms, small and great.

Transgenerational family heritage in business was a one-of-a-kind and important relationship for generations to capitalize on for starting and maintaining a business in the long run. Without this social capital, a business would be underdeveloped in the short run.

In the context of business as ministry for the common good, relationships play a pivotal role as a form of social capital. Karen's case illustrates this, where her relationship with her grandfather, a stakeholder in Karen Family Farm, not only facilitated her geographical and professional transitions but also inspired philanthropic actions like donating land to the Iowa Natural Heritage Foundation. This exemplifies how relationships, especially those rooted in family and transgenerational heritage, are integral in fostering social capital that contributes to both business development and broader societal wellbeing. Transgenerational family heritage in business as ministry was a one-of-a-kind and important relationship for generations to capitalize on for starting and maintaining a business in the long run. Without this social capital, a business as ministry would be underdeveloped in the short run.

Trust

In this study, trust—a vital component of social capital—had a substantial influence on how a profit-making business was executed as a Christian ministry. A Deborah Salon client, Emma, praised the establishment for caring for people's tousles and souls. It was a live rendition of business as ministry. Deborah earned the trust of her business stakeholders by practicing servanthood. Tan (2006) defines servanthood as a selfless attitude toward life that emphasizes putting others' needs ahead of your own. Those who practice servanthood as a ministry in business have a Christlike heart to serve rather than to be served.

Rebuilding the trust that was once lost is one of the most difficult missions for individuals, organizations, communities, or even nations because it requires a fundamental shift in perception and behavior. Trust is a complex psychological construct built over time through consistent positive interactions and experiences. When trust is broken, it creates a perception of betrayal, dishonesty, or incompetence, which can deeply damage relationships and institutions (Dirks & Ferrin, 2001). One of the negative approaches to rebuilding trust is to use one's legitimate or financial power to demand immediate forgiveness or reconciliation. Another negative approach to rebuilding trust is fear, intimidation, or pressure tactics. These tactics will only exacerbate the situation and create an atmosphere of fear and distrust, making it even more challenging to restore trust (Kramer & Pittinsky, 2012).

At Catholic Worker Community Farm, forgiveness and reconciliation of Godhuman, human-human, and human-nature relationships were regarded as challenging spiritual battles that required the letting go of egos and pride. Christian faith-based rebuilding trust was exercised with the example of how God forgave each of us while we were still sinners and Jesus Christ as the mediator. The setting was for two farmworkers to practice forgiveness and reconciliation through working together under the sunlight and surrounded by nature, weeding or harvesting, for example. It was preferred for the two participants of the exercise to have a minimum influence from their legitimate or financial power to each other. It was discovered that engaging in congruent communication while basking in the sun by exchanging stories was an exceptionally peaceful and restorative experience. David and Barbara's gardening experience exemplified how they might exercise forgiveness and reconciliation by restoring their relationship with God and nature. This one-of-a-kind experience and perspective helped to create and rebuild trust with others.

According to study participants Christopher and George, openness and appreciation with humility and honesty were the keys to establishing and maintaining trust. Telling and listening to stories from one another were the lubricant and catalyst in the restoration and reconciliation of the trust.

In brief, trust is not only a fundamental principle of Christianity but also a crucial element for building social capital in business as ministry. By consistently practicing servanthood and forgiveness, businesses as a ministry can foster deep and trusting relationships with their stakeholders, which will ultimately contribute to the common good.

Goodwill

In this study, goodwill, a critical component of social capital, had a considerable impact on the operational performance of business as ministry. Hardworking is an element of the Midwestern culture in America. It is a way in which businesses build their reputations. Living in voluntary poverty in the twenty-first century exemplified the US rural Midwestern Christian culture like no other.

Is voluntary poverty poor or rich? What is the richness of voluntary poverty? According to the Catholic Worker Movement, voluntary poverty is a lifestyle in which people choose to live more simply and renounce material comfort and luxury in order to serve God more effectively. This lifestyle involves an ongoing search to define what is necessary and possible. It is a conscious protest against injustice by choosing to live together with those who are materially poor.

The idea of voluntary poverty is not to be poor but to be rich in other ways. By living a life of voluntary poverty, people can focus on the things that matter most to them, such as family, friends, and community. They can also focus on their spiritual growth and development, creating a greater sense of purpose and fulfillment.

Therefore, voluntary poverty is a goodwill of the Catholic Worker Community

Farm and thus is a rich social capital of the enterprise.

In summary, this study has demonstrably linked the critical social capital component of goodwill, exemplified by the practice of voluntary poverty within the Catholic Worker Community Farm, to enhanced operational performance within the realm of business as ministry for the common good. This seemingly paradoxical notion of voluntary poverty as a source of richness, both spiritual and practical, lies at the heart of this connection. By prioritizing shared values, communal living, and service over material accumulation, the Community Farm fostered a unique and potent form of social capital, one that demonstrably strengthened its operational effectiveness and aligned it with its higher purpose of serving the common good. This study's findings offered valuable insights for other faith-based enterprises seeking to leverage the power of goodwill and voluntary poverty to achieve both spiritual and material success.

Cooperation

This study found that cooperation, which is an essential element of social capital, significantly influenced the operational effectiveness of business as ministry. Cooperation is possible when human dignity is respected. The belief of the Catholic Worker Community Farm behind equality was Christian personalism. According to Mary, the farm's founder recognizes and celebrates the dignity of each individual. The organizational hierarchy was flattened. The consensus decision-making system was actualized. Stakeholders were welcome to join the monthly leadership meeting to contribute their unique talent and insight to the decision-making process. The consensus system was a valuable decisionmaking platform in communities like Catholic Worker Community Farm, which valued inclusiveness and cooperation. It might aid in developing consensus and support for decisions, as well as the development of more creative and inventive solutions and forming a more cohesive and inclusive community. Though, some difficulties were encountered with this system as well. The consensus system might be time-consuming, making it difficult to establish consensus on all subjects and manage conflict and disagreement. As a result, it required individuals to devote their time and energy to make it work.

The business outcome of William Conservation Farm revealed that cooperation with other businesses, non-profit organizations, and government agencies to share resources, expertise, and knowledge contributed to its social capital to establish a supportive and collaborative work environment for the common good.

In summary, fostering a culture of inclusivity and cooperation through conscious decision-making processes like the one employed at Catholic Worker Community Farm served as a valuable model for businesses seeking to integrate social capital into their business as ministry for the common good. While challenges like time constraints and managing conflict may arise, the potential benefits of increased employee engagement, creative solutions, and a more cohesive community can ultimately contribute to a more effective and impactful organization.

Intellectual Capital

Intellectual capital refers to the collective intangible assets possessed by an organization, encompassing the intellectual properties, knowledge, skills, and creative abilities of its organizational and operational people, as well as the value of its organizational brand, procedures, and systems (Shafique et al., 2021; Sveiby, 1997).

According to Marr (2018), the presence of intellectual capital within an organization plays a crucial role in determining its overall sustainability. This is because companies have the ability to utilize their intellectual capital in order to generate value for their stakeholders through the development of new products and services, enhancing operational efficiency, and attaining sustainability.

Creativity

According to Paul, a study participant who fostered his children's creativity by delegating the production and management of the Paul Family Farm YouTube channel to them, creativity is both nature and nurture. Study participant Lisa regarded creativity as a green thumb and the ability to listen and tell stories. Growing lives with new ideas and solutions, as well as finding new and innovative ways to impact the lives of others, positively contributed to the intellectual capital of the farm. David, another study participant, suggested practicing creativity rather than talking about creativity. He believed creativity could be fostered through practice.

In brief, the findings of this study provided compelling insights into the multifaceted nature of creativity as a driving force for intellectual capital in business as ministry. Just as nurturing children's creativity on the Paul Family Farm fostered innovation and a sense of purpose, so too can businesses leverage creative approaches to problem-solving, storytelling, and community engagement to serve the common good effectively. By embracing a spirit of experimentation and listening to diverse voices, businesses can cultivate a culture of creativity that fuels both their intellectual capital and their positive impact on the world.

Insight

According to <u>Cambridge Dictionary (n.d.)</u>, insight is the ability to comprehend something's deeper meaning or significance. It entails looking beyond the surface and perceiving things from a different perspective.

William, the farm owner of William Conservation Farm, used his insight to identify the community's needs, especially those of his farmer, and devised programs and services to satisfy those needs. Daniel, the farmer who rented the farmland from the William family, has worked with William for many years to impact the community and the world positively. Insight, according to William, is life-long learning knowledge.

In summary, the findings in this study eloquently captured the essence of insight as a cornerstone of intellectual capital in business as ministry. William, the farm owner, exemplifies how deep understanding of community needs can be gleaned from careful observation and a willingness to look beyond the surface. As the findings suggested, this insight formed the bedrock for effective programs and services that uplifted not just individuals but the entire community. By nurturing a culture of curiosity, empathy, and active listening, business as ministry can harness the power of insight to serve the common good with greater effectiveness and purpose.

Brand

According to K. L. Keller and Swaminathan (2019), A brand is valuable because it embodies a collection of intangible resources that may be used to produce income, draw in and keep consumers, and provide long-term benefits. An organization's long-term plan outlining how to promote itself to its target market and accomplish its objectives is known as its brand strategy. It guides the creation of a powerful, recognizable brand that will connect with customers and sustain company growth.

In this study, corporate brands served as the firms' personalities based on concepts such as humanizing the business, authenticity, consistency, emotional connection, and uniqueness. Participating enterprises' strong brand reputation attracted and retained interns, farm workers, customers, and community partners with positive word-of-mouth promotions. The fact that the soil at the Catholic Worker Community Farm was perceived as beautiful and powerful suggested that the brand's value for soil is more than just dirt. Elizabeth Tailor positioned itself as a slow fashion brand. It required braveries to differentiate from the prevalent trend of fast fashion to create its brand value. The courage itself was a brand. William Conservation Farm increased its brand value by portraying itself as a custodian of farmland water and soil conservation, as well as via community involvement. William Conservation Farm has established a leading position in farmland conservation technologies by partnering with local research and development institutes. Its brand worth was its reputation. Its brand value was the difference between what the farm would be worth without its brand and what it is worth with its brand.

In conclusion, the study's findings illuminated the profound potential of a brand as a powerful tool for intellectual capital within business as ministry. Just as the Catholic Worker Community Farm leverages its reputation for soil stewardship and community engagement to attract farmworkers and build trust, so too can businesses cultivate brands that embody their values and social capital. A strong brand, grounded in authenticity and a commitment to the common good, can serve as an intangible asset, attracting customers, investors, and talent while simultaneously amplifying a business's positive impact on the world. By prioritizing transparency, ethical practices, and genuine community engagement, businesses can craft brands that not only generate economic value but also contribute meaningfully to the intellectual capital of the common good.

Systems

Concerning the organizational structure of farms examined in this study, familyowned and operated agriculture systems, and community-supported agriculture systems existed on a macro level.

Family-owned and operated farms generally had a modest to moderate scale, frequently characterized by intergenerational succession. The family members were responsible for making significant choices regarding the property. The collaborative engagement of family members in farming was a prevalent phenomenon when the farm assumed a central role as a defining aspect of the family's lifestyle.

Several advantages were associated with the ownership and operation of agriculture by families. Family farmers frequently exhibited higher commitment towards their land and livestock than corporate farmers. Family farms were more inclined towards sustainability due to their reduced likelihood of engaging in environmentally harmful practices.

Nevertheless, family-owned and operated farms encountered various problems. Family farms were frequently characterized by their comparatively smaller size and lower level of efficiency in comparison to corporate farms. This phenomenon could pose challenges for family farmers regarding pricing competitiveness compared to corporate farms. Family farms were additionally susceptible to economic downturns.

Notwithstanding the obstacles, family-owned and operated agriculture remained significant in the American Midwest economy and society. Family farms played a crucial role in supplying the American population with fresh and nutritious food while simultaneously contributing to the preservation of rural communities and their cultural heritage in the Midwest of the United States.

Operating a family farm provided the Paul family with a tangible illustration of business as ministry in the rural Midwestern region of the United States. People, business, ministry, financial, agricultural, livestock, gardening, social media, and homeschooling systems were present. The components and processes of these systems were interconnected and operated in concert for the common good.

Community-supported agriculture systems were an excellent means of bolstering local agricultural producers while promoting fresh and nutritious food consumption. Additionally, these platforms allowed consumers to enhance their understanding of the origins and cultivation methods employed in producing their food. Consumers could connect with the farmers responsible for cultivating their food, thus contributing to conserving the local community's agricultural legacy.

These systems might contribute to intellectual capital because they aligned Christian ministry and business goals, enhanced stewardship of resources, promoted transparency and accountability, positively impacted the community, and enabled sustainable growth. In general, the intellectual capital of organizational systems of business as ministry is derived from embodying the organization's expertise, knowledge, and procedures that support its objectives, innovation, efficiency, and long-term viability (Xi, 2021). A business as ministry can generate value for all stakeholders and accomplish its long-term strategic objectives by investing in and efficiently managing its systems.

Conceptualization of the Findings

The conceptualizations of the findings that arose in this study are as follows: First, business as ministry proved that it is possible to integrate faith and business, as well as business and ministry, in a way that is both sustainable and beneficial to society. This concept challenges the long-held belief that the sacred and the secular were distinct domains. Second, business as ministry conceptualizes that the objective of business is to serve God and others rather than just to make money, i.e., the purpose of business as ministry is not profit but the common good. This concept challenges the usual notion of business as purely profit-driven. Third, by demonstrating that business can be a way of serving God and others, business as ministry can assist in reinvigorating a sense of vocation in the workplace. Employees may have a more fulfilling and meaningful work life as a result of this. Fourth, by reframing the evaluation model of corporate capital under the common good treasure model, business as ministry can contribute to the establishment of a more humane economy. This concept has the potential to result in a more just and equal society in the world, as well as a more sustainable ecosystem on earth.

How the Findings Agreed With the Literature

Rourke (1996) claimed that the common good consists of both a formal and a material part. Friendship, communion, citizenship, harmony, peace, integrity, compassion, and other quality terms that do not diminish when split and scattered among many might thus be shared as a formal part of the common good. A material part of the common good is a quantitative expression indicating that the efficacy of a good is determined by how it is divided and distributed. Once divided, it will shrink. It can also be substituted by the same amount of a similar good, such as natural resources, products, or services. The perspectives of business as ministry stakeholders in the rural United States Midwest agreed with this categorization and expanded on it with more nuanced meaning of the common good treasure grouping. Spiritual, social, intellectual, and financial capital are transcended into the common good treasure.

McVea and Naughton (2021) focused on the concept of the common good of business, drawing upon the definitions and inspiration provided by the Caritas in Veritate (CV) and Catholic Social Teachings (CST). Their studies emphasized the significance of "the total of social conditions" (p. 6). The authors contend that a well-functioning firm produces "three interdependent sets of goods" that provide affluent aspects to the common good of business: "good goods, good work, and good wealth." The results of this study elaborated on the findings of McVea and Naughton (2021), showing the comprehensive range of societal factors. Additionally, it argued that a proficient organization generates four interconnected categories of resources, namely spiritual capital, social capital, intellectual capital, and financial capital, collectively referred to as the common good treasure, which contribute to the prosperity of the business.

Wong and Rae (2011) claimed that the intrinsic worth of business lies in its intrinsic purpose of engaging in transformational service for the common good. According to Van Duzer (2010), the intrinsic purpose of a business encompasses the generation of wealth through the production of goods and services, as well as the promotion of human wellbeing through employment. These elements are considered the primary objectives of a business. Additionally, Van Duzer (2010) posits that fostering relationships and contributing to community development are secondary objectives of a business. Van Duzer (2010) claimed:

> There are two legitimate, first-order, intrinsic purposes of business. As stewards of God's creation, business leaders should manage their businesses (1) to provide the community with goods and services that will enable it to flourish and (2) to provide opportunities for meaningful work to allow employees to express their God-given

creativity. Nurturing relationships and community-building are critical to healthy businesses. They are not its reason for being; they don't rise to the level of a foundational purpose (pp. 42–43).

The findings of this study align with the conclusions drawn by Wong and Rae

(2011)   regarding the intrinsic nature of business. Additionally, the study expands upon Van Duzer's (2010) framework of two primary and two secondary objectives of business, by incorporating the concept of the common good treasure. This treasure encompasses the spiritual, social, intellectual, and financial capitals when viewed from a resources' perspective. The legitimate objective of business as ministry can then be seen as the optimization of the common good treasure for the benefit of society as a whole. Within the framework of this business as ministry paradigm, the process of determining the specific product or service to be developed and produced revolves around evaluating the various options available to the company in order to ascertain which of these options would optimize the common good treasure. In order to enhance the common good treasure, it is imperative to effectively integrate the spiritual, social, intellectual, and financial capital resources, ensuring a balanced and sustainable collaboration. This necessitates adopting an approach in the pursuit of the common good equilibrium, i.e., God's equilibrium, while also embracing a vision and mission of treasure sharing.

From a scientific standpoint, the research project on the science of gratitude by the Greater Good Science Center at the University of California,

Berkeley, revealed that gratitude is an inherent component of the human experience (Algoe & Way, 2014). Several studies have also identified genes that may contribute to human gratitude. Gratitude is both nature and nurture (Allen, 2018). The emergence of gratitude is witnessed in children as they advance through their early stages of growth and development (Allen, 2018). The correlation between employee personality and organizational culture is evident (C.-C. Lin, 2015; Liu et al., 2017). According to their findings, individuals who prayed for others were more grateful. The study indicated a potential correlation between spirituality and dispositional appreciation (Lambert et al., 2009). According to A. M. Grant and Gino (2010), gratitude serves as a motivating factor for individuals, leading them to exhibit increased levels of compassion, kindness, and helpfulness.

Additionally, expressing gratitude has been found to enhance the quality of relationships and potentially contribute to a more positive workplace environment. The present study utilized the coding of family histories to corroborate the findings reported by the Greater Good Science Center at the University of California, Berkeley. The qualitative analysis of family narratives consistently indicates a significant genetic influence and attachment effect on the transgenerational transmission of family heritage in domains such as faith, farming, and business. Christian faith has been a guiding force for business as ministry as they navigated many challenges and achievements. This is accomplished through the expression of gratitude, wherein businesspeople give honor to God, express appreciation, and prioritize serving others without seeking personal benefit. The explicit inclusion of gratitude within the framework of the common good served as a motivating factor for participants in the present study, leading them to exhibit heightened levels of compassion, kindness, and helpfulness, thus fostering the development and fortification of interpersonal relationships. They consistently employed their ample financial capital as a catalyst to develop their spiritual, social, and intellectual capital.

How the Findings Contributed to the Scholarship

Rundle and Lee (2022) used a survey study to identify four distinct groups of BAM practitioners in order to understand better the human and contextual factors that contribute to the efficacy and sustainability of a BAM enterprise. The study employed missional and business identities to generate a two-dimensional matrix. "BAMers" ("High" in missional and "High" in business), "Evangelists" ("High" in missional and "Low" in business), FaithDriven Entrepreneurs (FDEs) ("Low" in missional and "High" in business), and "Explorers" ("Low" in missional and "Low" in business) were identified as the four types of BAM practitioners (p. 425–429). The study's most notable finding is that BAM practitioners with varying social identities have proportionally different ideas of how each of the four "bottom lines" of economic, social, spiritual, and environmental impact should be prioritized. FDEs favor economic outcomes over spiritual consequences, Evangelists prefer spiritual outcomes over economic outcomes, BAMers are balanced, and Explorers are imbalanced. Based on their social identity, job experience, and management practices, the typological model predicts significant differences in how BAM practitioners "do mission" and "do business" (Rundle & Lee, 2022, p. 436).

The current study transferred the aforementioned research findings to the context of business as ministry in rural areas of the Midwestern United States. It drew upon the findings reported by the Greater Good Science Center at the University of California, Berkeley, from their research project on the science of gratitude, as well as the principles of attachment theory in developmental psychology. The paradigm was expanded to encompass the integration of missiology, neuroscience, and developmental psychology. The attachment theory was employed due to its relevance in exploring how human nature might be nurtured.

Similarly, the identity of a faith-driven entrepreneur is associated with a transgenerational family heritage in the realm of business. Furthermore, the identity of a BAMer emerges when *both* the evangelist and entrepreneur identities are prominent, and it is connected to a transgenerational family heritage encompassing *both* faith and business.

The "Explorer" identity is recognized when *both* the evangelist and entrepreneur identities are simultaneously inconspicuous, a phenomenon commonly associated with the absence of transgenerational family lineage in *either* faith *or* business domains. The identity formation process is multifaceted and subject to the combined effects of *both* nature and nurture (Erikson, 1968; Harris & Mireles-Rios, 2021; Monrouxe, 2016). The concept of nature pertains to the genetic and biological elements that influence our identity, whereas nurture encompasses the environmental variables that shape our identity. In the current study, the data obtained from the study participants supported the assertion made by Rundle and Lee (2022). The present study observed a prevalence of the BAMer identity among the sampled individuals. This can be attributed to the fact that farmers typically inherit a family tradition of entrepreneurship in farming.

Hence, in order to establish a sustainable business as mission (BAM) enterprise over a long term, it is advantageous to have a transgenerational family heritage that encompasses both a commitment to mission-driven faith and a background in entrepreneurship. This serves as a necessary condition for a sustainable BAM business. Developing a strong BAMer identity is also deemed sufficient to meet the requirements for a thriving BAM business. A practitioner of BAM business is more inclined to exhibit characteristics of an "Evangelist" who comes from a transgenerational family heritage rooted solely in the missional faith tradition.

In contrast, it is more probable that a practitioner of BAM business would assume the role of a faith-driven entrepreneur whose family lineage is primarily associated with business endeavors across generations. Faith-driven entrepreneurs may encounter more challenges when engaging in missional ministries than their company operations experiences. Therefore, it may be advisable for those "Explorers" seeking to cultivate a missional identity and draw upon their family heritage in both missional faith and entrepreneurship to consider engaging in short-term missions or a BAM pilot project.

The Common Good Treasure

In their empirical study, Sorenson and Milbrandt (2023) sought to examine the association between family faith, family values, business family social capital, and business outcome in the specific setting of family-owned enterprises. The study introduced the concept of family social capital. As per the authors' perspective, family social capital is defined as the collection of resources within familial connections and can be utilized to achieve individual, familial, and business goals. The authors' findings suggested that family faith has a beneficial influence on family values. These values, in turn, contribute to developing social capital within business families, specifically through fostering trust, facilitating communication, and promoting commitment. Furthermore, the accumulation of social capital within business families can lead to several favorable outcomes, including the sustainable succession of family businesses, improved business performance, and increased community support.

The present study incorporated the notion of family social capital as a reference frame for constant comparison during the thematic coding process in order to explore its implications and applications. The coding of research participants' narratives yielded four key themes of spiritual, social, intellectual, and financial capital concerning the research questions of this study. Wisdom, values, culture, and ministry are all components of spiritual capital. Social capital is comprised of relationships, trust, goodwill, and cooperation. Creativity, insight, brand, and system constitute intellectual capital. Profit, cash, debt, and asset categories were coded as financial capital. This finding revealed that business as ministry has its own spiritual, social, intellectual, and financial capital to contribute to the common good. As a result, the summation of financial, spiritual, social, and intellectual capital is "The Common Good Treasure" (see Figure 5).

The Business as Ministry Model

This inquiry pertains to a business model for establishing and administrating business as ministry for the common good. The SWM model emphasized the accumulation of financial capital for the benefit of shareholders, whereas the ST model emphasized the organization's social responsibilities. Scholars have proposed an alternative framework called the Common Good (CG) model in response to the prevailing business models (Felber, 2019; McVea & Naughton, 2021; Rieger, 2015; Rourke, 1996; Sison & Fontrodona, 2011, 2013; Turnbull, 2018; Van Duzer, 2010; Wong & Rae, 2011). Although there were several proposals regarding the CG model, they all shared a common theme: under the SWM model, profit was the principal objective of a for-profit business. However, under the CG model, the profit of a profit-making business was regarded as a means to an end of the common good. The business as ministry model further developed the CG model's idea of placing the common good as the ultimate purpose of a profit-making business into an operating system by entailing the concept of the common good treasure, encompassing the following four main themes: spiritual, social, intellectual, and financial capital, emerged in this study, as illustrated in Table 6.

The business as ministry model functions as a resource-based operating system, as Figure 6 depicts. Its primary objective is to establish and grow the common good treasure across spiritual, social, intellectual, and financial domains. By exhaustively encompassing the primary facets of a profit-making enterprise, these four domains furnish business stakeholders with a systematic overview and strategic approach to business administration. Under the business as ministry model, the decision regarding which product or service to produce or provide is determined according to the business as ministry model by assessing which alternative optimizes the common good treasure. In light of the organization's intrinsic capabilities and available resources, it is the responsibility of the enterprise's management to devise a plan for the most efficient distribution of resources in order to deliver products and services efficiently. By adopting the business as ministry model, the ideal balance of spiritual, social, intellectual, and financial capital can be achieved, which in turn promotes the sustainability of the planet Earth, human flourishing, and the glory of God.

Based on the operating system of business administration, gaining insights through the common good treasure assessment enables the organizational management to address inquiries pertaining to the purpose, market, and resources, including but not limited to the following:

The purpose:

- What are our fundamental beliefs regarding Christian faith in the context of entrepreneurship and stewardship?

- What are the Christian values that are prevalent in the realm of business as ministry?

- What are the vision and missions of our business as ministry based on our Christian values?

- What strategies can be employed to enhance the efficiency and effectiveness of our organization's CGT?

- What is the most effective method for sharing our CGT with individuals who are in need?

- What type of leadership and organizational culture should be cultivated?

The market:

- In which community are we currently situated?

- Which market segment should we consider entering?

- What is the optimal positioning strategy for our products and services in the targeted market segment?

- What strategies can effectively market and promote our products and services?

- What are the locations available to our business and ministry?

- What pricing strategies should be employed to sustain profitability for our products and services?

- What are the desired characteristics of individuals we aspire to collaborate with?

The resources:

- What are the available sustainable resources at our disposal?
- What is the evaluation of the common good treasure that our firm has

  and aims to achieve in terms of spiritual, social, intellectual, and

  financial capital?

- What products and services are within the scope of our design and

  build capabilities?

- What structures, methods, procedures, and systems can our
  organization adopt?

As a tool, the business as ministry model can be used in business

administration to foster harmonious relationships between God and humanity,

among individuals, and between humanity and nature.

Summary of Discussion

The coding of research participants' narratives yielded four key themes

of spiritual, social, intellectual, and financial capital concerning the research

questions. Wisdom, values, culture, and ministry categories were coded as

spiritual capital. Social capital is comprised of relationships, trust, goodwill,

and cooperation. Creativity, insight, brand, and systems constitute intellectual

capital. Profit, cash, debt, and assets are all components of financial capital.

The findings revealed that business as ministry has its own spiritual, social,

intellectual, and financial capital to contribute to the common good. As a

result, the common good treasure was conceptualized as the optimal

integration of spiritual, social, intellectual, and financial capital, as shown in

Figure 5. Consequently, the business as ministry model was developed through the integration of the common good treasure into the core of the

resource-based operating system of the business administration (see Table 6

and Figure 6). The subsequent chapter will expound upon the implications of

the business

as ministry model.

Chapter 7

Implications and Conclusions

This basic qualitative study aimed to understand how the business as ministry stakeholders in the rural Midwestern United States practiced and perceived business as ministry for the common good. In this chapter, the implications of the business as ministry model will be elaborated. Furthermore, I will consider avenues for future research and deliver a concluding remark for this study.

Implications

The primary understanding that emerged from this study was that business as ministry possesses its own spiritual, social, intellectual, and financial capital, which it uses to advance the common good, according to the findings of this study. Consequently, the notion of the common good treasure emerged as the most effective amalgamation of spiritual, social, intellectual, and financial capital. As a result, the business as ministry model was established by incorporating the common good treasure into the core of the resource-based operating system of the business administration.

Theoretical Implications

The findings gave rise to a number of theoretical implications. The results obtained from this research were consistent with and made a valuable contribution to pertinent body of literature.

The "Why" Versus the "What and How"

While previous research focused on business as ministry for the common good in the domain of the "why" (McVea & Naughton, 2021; Nichols, 1989; Sison & Fontrodona, 2011, 2013), this study extended to the realm of the "what and how," specifically in terms of business administration, ranging from vision and mission statements to corporate strategy and operational processes. In the literature, concepts such as "intrinsic purpose of business," "priorities," "quadruple bottom lines," or "the common good" answered "why" domain inquiries such as "What is the goal we are trying to achieve?" "What problem are we trying to solve?" that is, "What bottom lines are we targeting to fulfill?" (Gort &

Tunehag, 2018; Van Duzer, 2010).

According to the study's findings, the concept of the common good treasure and the business as ministry model attended to inquiries in the "what and how" domain, such as "What sustainable resources do we have to achieve the goals set forth in our vision and mission statements?" "What needs to be done?" "How will we do it?" "What are the best practices that our business as ministry can adopt in terms of creating and growing our spiritual, social, intellectual, and financial capital?" The question is, "What are the potential challenges and contingencies?" For business as ministry, the questions "why," "what," and "how" are complementary. As a result, the findings of this study contributed to the body of literature in a complementary manner.

Ethics-Based Versus Resource-Based

The majority of current research highlighted the importance of values, ethics, and moral considerations in business decisions, as well as a belief in a greater purpose beyond profit maximization, emphasizing stakeholder well-being, and developing a sense of community inside the enterprise. Long-term considerations, social effect, and sustainability led decisions rather than short-term financial advantages, with transformational leadership that inspired and motivated people via shared values and a sense of purpose.

According to the study's findings, the concept of the common good treasure may help to acquire a sustainable advantage by conducting a strategic analysis of internal and external resources in terms of spiritual, social, intellectual, and financial capital. The business as ministry model may assist in identifying and leveraging core strengths, building and managing essential resources, and altering to shifting market conditions. Decisions in a resource-based strategy may be guided by resource availability, potential for value generation, and optimal integration of common good treasure with strategic leadership focused on optimizing resource allocation, creating efficiencies, and meeting performance goals. Complementarily, the results of this study made a contribution to the existing body of literature.

A Design Platform Versus an Operating System

The previous research on business as ministry for the common good served as a design platform for business as ministry operating system design (McVea & Naughton, 2021; Sison & Fontrodona, 2012; Van Duzer, 2010).

The existing literature provided a direction, guidelines, tools, and functionalities necessary for the design of an operating system.

The result of the present study provided insight into the design of an operating system to provide the underlying infrastructure and tools necessary for the smooth operation of an organization's core processes and functions. In a complementary manner, the findings of this study added to the extant corpus of knowledge.

Practical Implications

The practical implications of the business as ministry model encompass the potential real-world applications. The author elucidates the potential applications of the study's findings in addressing practical challenges or enhancing current methodologies. The significance of practical implications lies in their ability to facilitate the connection between academic knowledge and real-world applications, enhancing research relevance for practitioners.

Family Farm

Consider the Paul Family Farm as an illustration; a concise CGT evaluation could be conducted as follows: The family believed that "Everything we do is for the glory of God." Family and service to others were two of their Christian values. Their sustainable resources were a faithful family of three generations, a medium scale of fertile farmland, John Deere equipment, two large size grain bins, a planted community church, and a YouTube channel. The family farm was in the Midwest of the United States, the heartland of American history, culture, and faith. They grew corn and

soybeans for the world and veggies and fresh milk for the family. They

served the community through the church they planted with Paul as the

pastor, provided financial assistance to a Indian missionary in

India, and maintained a YouTube channel where they shared their faithful life

experiences. They also had a small online business offering souvenirs of their

family farm. However, they did not ask for donations on their YouTube

channel. They were rich in spiritual and social capital in terms of CGT. In

terms of intellectual capital, the family had generations of farming expertise

and experience. In terms of financial capital, the farm was high in fixed

assets but low in cash. The family focused on creating a self-sufficient and

selfsustaining ecosystem to optimize their CGT.

Following the CGT evaluation, a market study can be performed to

examine the business climate and the communities served by the ministry.

The second question that may be asked is: "What would be an optimal

integration of spiritual, social, intellectual, and financial capital for

sustainable business and ministry for the common good according to the

business as ministry model?" If the leadership prioritized social, financial,

spiritual, and intellectual capital as the priority of their CGT, for example, the

resource allocation should be optimized in the following order: relationships,

trust, goodwill, and cooperation; profit, cash, debt, and assets; wisdom,

values, culture, and ministry; creativity, insight, brand, and systems. Finally,

from the market study, match and map these objectives with the market and community needs to generate a business as ministry strategy, and then plan and execute the family, agricultural, and ministerial operations in accordance with the strategy.

Community Farm

Consider the Catholic Worker Community Farm as another example. The farm's founders believed in the Catholic Worker Movement, voluntary simplicity and poverty, Christian personalism, and social justice. Their Christian values included forgiveness, gratitude, humility, honesty, trust, integrity, love, respect, and service to others. What sustainable resources they had were a servantship team including the founders, small scale of fertile farmland, gardening equipment, a well-established network and a good reputation in the community, and 15 years of expertise running a CSA community farm. The farm was in the heartland of American history, culture, and faith. They grew fresh fruits and vegetables for the community. They served the community by offering opportunities to work on the farm to experience the connections with people and the nature, the voluntary simplicity, and voluntary poverty. Farmworkers, on the other hand, were not paid.

Founders, farm managers, and interns were compensated with in-farm lodging and board, while other farmworkers were compensated with a box of fresh farm produce for every three hours of farm work in a week during the growing season. The farm was rich in spiritual, social, and intellectual capital but modest in financial capital. Farm workers were thus primarily compensated with spiritual and social capital, specifically by positioning the community farm services on green therapy, soil therapy, and safe therapy in the market segment of "connection to nature and connection to people." To optimize their CGT, the farm aimed to develop a healthy CSA ecosystem with social justice in food and the psychological well-being of community members to build a servanthood culture in the community farm to optimize their CGT.

Analogous to the business as ministry of a family farm, a market analysis can be undertaken subsequent to the CGT assessment to scrutinize the business environment and the communities that the ministry serves. Another question that can be inquired about is "What would be an optimal integration of spiritual, social, intellectual, and financial capital for sustainable business and ministry for the common good according to the business as ministry model?" In the event that the leadership establishes spiritual, social, intellectual, and financial capital as the priority of concerns for the farm's CGT, for instance, the allocation of resources ought to be optimized as follows: wisdom, values, culture, and ministry; relationships, trust, goodwill, and cooperation; creativity; creativity, insight, brand, and systems; profit, cash, debt, and assets. Ultimately, formulate a business as ministry strategy by matching and mapping these objectives with market and community needs as determined by the market research. Subsequently, organize and carry out the CSA and ministerial implementation in alignment with the strategy.

Niche Business

Elizabeth Tailor and Joseph Medinformatics, both discovered themselves to be intellectual capital affluent in this study. Joseph and his partners owned a proprietary intellectual property in computational medical informatics technology. The exceptional intellectual capital was applied towards the development of spiritual and financial capital. A corporate strategy could be formulated by conducting an analysis of the requirements of medical practitioners and patients in accordance with the business as ministry model. This analysis would involve prioritizing the intellectual, financial, spiritual, and social capital (CGT) in that order, followed by the following resource allocation priorities: creativity, insight, brand, and systems; profit, cash, debt, and assets; wisdom, values, culture, and ministry; relationships, trust, goodwill, and cooperation. Following this, the corporate strategy could be implemented in a sustainable manner.

Elizabeth Tailor developed its brand value by positioning its products and services at the opposite end of the fast fashion industry, namely slow fashion. While fast fashion buyers were looking for stylish and economical clothing, slow fashion customers were more conservative and environmentally conscious. Elizabeth, the primary sustainable resource, was a fashion design college graduate with an agricultural and Christian religious family tradition. Such a differentiated advantage in resources best fits the market and community culture in the rural Midwestern United States for a sustainable business as ministry.

Coding from Elizabeth might be used to summarize the study's implications. "You don't have to be rich to have a comfortable life," Elizabeth contended. When her perception was translated into CGT language, it became, "You don't have to be financially rich to be God's beloved children." A healthy and sustained business as ministry does not need a maximum on financial capital, but rather an optimal integration of spiritual, social, intellectual, and financial capital—an optimal CGT."

Future Research

The initial iteration of the business as ministry model was derived from the findings of the current qualitative research. Further study is required to explore the theoretical associations elucidated in this study. Random samples in alternative contexts can be employed to ascertain the transferability, applicability, and constraints of the proposed business model. For instance, additional studies could ascertain potential disparities between the concepts of business as ministry and business as mission within the rural and urban contexts or between the cultural contexts of the US Midwest and Silicon Valley.

The exploration of methodology for enhancing spiritual, social, intellectual, and financial capital might have been widely investigated within the relevant academic fields. Nevertheless, there is still a need to research the manner in which the various elements of the common good treasure, specifically spiritual, social, intellectual, and financial capital, can be efficiently coordinated and collaboratively aligned to optimize the common good treasure. Furthermore, it is worth considering the possibility of future research that might center on the development of an algorithmic methodology for assessing the spiritual, social, intellectual, and financial capital, as well as exploring their practical applications within this field. This study has the potential to serve as a foundational framework for future research attempts.

Another area of future research could be constructing and implementing a market analysis framework within the business as ministry model. A market analysis is a thorough examination of the current market that assists businesses in understanding the volume and value of the market, potential customer segments and their purchasing behavior, the positions of players in the same segment, and the overall economic and community environment, including entry barriers and industry or state regulations. Just as when temperature, moisture, and oxygen are optimal, the seed of a business as ministry theory would be ready for breaking the soil when the purpose, resources, and market analysis are in place.

Conclusions

The fundamental understanding of this study was that stakeholders in the rural Midwestern United States who supported business as ministry believed that the organization possesses spiritual, social, intellectual, and financial capital resources that could be utilized for the common good. The present exposition of the common good treasure concept and the business as ministry model is based on well-established scholarly literature, recognized qualitative research methodologies, and the findings derived from the data analysis of this basic qualitative research. Based on the common good treasure concept and the business as ministry model, a purpose and resource analysis methodology was developed for business as ministry. This methodology offers valuable insights into the optimization of the common good treasure to achieve sustainable entrepreneurial and ministerial outcomes for business as ministry. The practical implications of this study, as well as the common good treasure concept and the business as ministry model, may aid

Christian entrepreneurs in comprehending and managing a business as a Christian ministry.

Furthermore, this research has made a significant contribution to the foundation for developing a potential theory of business as ministry, which could include an analysis of its purpose, resources, and market.